Just Being There Makes The Difference!

Providing Care to the Sick, Disabled and

their Caregivers

Zelda E. Moore

Nurturing Care Publishing

Just Being There Makes the Difference
By Zelda E. Moore
Copyright © 2014

Nurturing Care Publishing

International Standard Book Number: 978-9906258-03

Cover Design: Maier Tudor

Unless otherwise indicated, all Scripture quotations are taken from *The Holy Bible: Authorized King James Version.* Italics in Scripture are for emphasis only.

Acknowledgments

To Louise and Howard Moore, MaMa and DayDay, although you did not live to see this book created, I thank you for the wonderful teachings you both instilled in me at an early age. You both saw that I was a nurturing, caring child and you made sure I embraced this trait. For this I am forever grateful.

I thank all the mentors throughout my life that molded me. I especially thank the following who encouraged and pushed me to write this book: Reverend, Doctor Cochran, President of Bethel Bible College and Seminary, Reverend Doctor Mary Gilmore, Bethel Bible College and Seminary, and my pastor, Reverend Doctor Stanley Hilton McClamb.

I thank God for this opportunity to serve and I am honored to be able to share the examples from my personal, work and research experiences.

Dedication

I give a special love filled thank you to my precious sister, Mrs. Annette Williams. Without the use of your business, AbleAnnie Administrative, to edit my book from the first word to the last it would have never existed. I love you Nette, not for what you do for me because you do it lovingly using the gifts God gave you. Anyone needing administrative services would be blessed by hiring your company.

I love you because we are more than sisters; we are friends, confidants, and more. You have always been there whenever I needed you for anything and even when it was uncomfortable for you God always helped you through. I cannot thank you enough.

Stephen, as Annette's husband, I thank you, my brother, I don't consider you as my brother in law because you are my brother in heart. You always support me and have always supported the sisterhood bond of the three "Moore Sisters" for this I give my love and thanks to you.

TABLE OF CONTENTS

Purpose

This book will give you the tools to begin your journey in providing ministerial care for the following situations:

1. People with a serious illness, terminal illness or new disability, as well as the persons caring for them
2. Times of grief
3. End of Life
4. Before and after the death support

You will also begin to explore the answers to these questions:

1. What is serious illness, end of life, terminal illness?
2. What does the Bible tell us?
3. What about the children?
4. How do I know what to do and say when I go to visit some one?
5. I am not comfortable doing visitation in a hospital is that wrong of me?

Chapter I

Why do we need to explore these topics?

The Bible tells us in Job14:1 "Man that is born of a woman is of few days and full of sorrow"[1]

Each one of us has been in a situation surrounding serious illness, death, dying, grief, and or care-giving. As Christian believers that are a part of the community of faith, we participate in hospital visitation, visits to the sick and shut in, attendance at wakes, memorials and funerals.

The Oxford English Dictionary[26] defines ministry as the spiritual work or service of any Christian or a group of

Christians, especially evangelists. A minister is defined as one who attends to the needs of others, a member of the clergy, men and woman licensed and or ordained for religious duties in the Christian Church. The Latin root for the English word minister means servant. For the purpose of this study I will use the word minister to mean any Christian that attends to the needs of those with an illness, visits the sick, or attends as a caregiver to someone who is ill or assists those who are caregivers to someone who is ill. I will use the same definition for minister for those who attend to those who are at the end –stage of physical life and those who are in grief.

The question is do we really know what to do, say or how to behave appropriately? How many of us avoid doing the ministry of the sick and shut in, and dying because of fear? The biblical account found in Job describes how Job's friends visited him during his long affliction and grief.

After hearing of his troubles were their words a comfort to Job or did they add to his misery?

Let's start with a story very familiar to most Christians, the story of Job:

Job 1:19; There was a man in the land of Uz, whose name *was* Job; and that man was perfect and upright, and one that feared God, and eschewed evil. And there were born unto him seven sons and three daughters. His substance also was seven thousand sheep, and three thousand camels, and five hundred yoke of oxen, and five hundred she asses, and a very great household; so that this man was the greatest of all the men of the east. And his sons went and feasted *in their* houses, everyone his day; and sent and called for their three sisters to eat and to drink with them. And it was so, when the days of *their* feasting were gone about, that Job sent and sanctified them, and rose up early in the morning, and offered burnt offerings *according* to the number of them all: for Job said, It may be that my sons have sinned, and cursed God in their hearts. Thus did Job continually. Now there was a day when the sons of God came to present themselves before the LORD, and Satan came also among them. And the LORD said unto Satan, Whence comest thou? Then Satan answered the LORD, and said, From going to and fro in the earth, and from walking up and down in it. And the LORD said unto Satan, Hast thou considered my servant Job, that *there is* none like him in the earth, a perfect and an upright man, one that feareth God, and escheweth evil? Then Satan answered the LORD, and said, Doth Job fear God for nought? Hast not thou made an hedge about him, and about his house, and about all that he hath on every side? thou hast blessed the work of his hands, and his substance is increased in the land. But put forth thine hand now, and touch all that he hath, and he will curse thee to thy face. And the LORD said unto Satan,

Behold, all that he hath *is* in thy power; only upon himself put not forth thine hand. So Satan went forth from the presence of the LORD. And there was a day when his sons and his daughters *were* eating and drinking wine in their eldest brother's house: And there came a messenger unto Job, and said, The oxen were plowing, and the asses feeding beside them: And the Sabeans fell *upon them*, and took them away; yea, they have slain the servants with the edge of the sword; and I only am escaped alone to tell thee.

While he *was* yet speaking, there came also another, and said, the fire of God is fallen from heaven, and hath burned up the sheep, and the servants, and consumed them; and I only am escaped alone to tell thee. While he *was* yet speaking, there came also another, and said, The Chaldeans made out three bands, and fell upon the camels, and have carried them away, yea, and slain the servants with the edge of the sword; and I only am escaped alone to tell thee.

While he *was* yet speaking, there came also another, and said, Thy sons and thy daughters *were* eating and drinking wine in their eldest brother's house: And, behold, there came a great wind from the wilderness, and smote the four corners of the house, and it fell upon the young men, and they are dead; and I only am escaped alone to tell thee.

Job 1:19 describes how the messengers came to inform Job that his animals and servants were killed, then here comes another to blurt out that others were burned, then his children. In my mind's eye I cannot see Job being his normal self or those around him not lamenting over the first servant's news when the next one comes without a blink or thought that maybe Job needs to process what has just been told to him before blurting out the next tragedy. Is the example found here in the book of Job a comforting way to tell someone such a series of horrible news? I think not. How would you react to such repeated news? Let's ponder on the persons we visit in the hospital week after week. For illustration Mrs. Smith goes to her family doctor's office on Friday because of a little pain in her stomach. He sends her to the hospital immediately for tests. Mrs. Smith arrives and the doctor doing the tests says she has to complete the consent so he can do the test. It says she could end up with an infection, need for surgery or sudden death; then Mrs. Smith wakes up from the test to be told she has cancer and they could not remove it but she will start chemotherapy and radiation therapy and by the way it will take all of her beautiful hair out; Mrs. Smith will have an ostomy bag after the surgery and will have to go to a skilled nursing home unless she has someone that can assist her with learning to do the ostomy bag and help her while she in on chemo; because she will be weak from being nauseous and vomiting. I made this a long running sentence on purpose. This is how the news can sound to those who are ill. Just like Job it is a long series of disturbing news. Most of us are not as faithful as Job so we as ministers to them must be there to assist with the avalanche of disturbing news. But the misery of Job does not end here just like it most likely does not end for Mrs. Smith.

Read on in Job 2:11- 13

Now when Job's three friends heard of all this evil that was come upon him, they came everyone from his own place; Eliphaz the Temanite, and Bildad the Shuhite, and Zophar the Naamathite: for they had made an appointment together to come to mourn with him and to comfort him. And when they lifted up their eyes afar off, and knew him not, they lifted up their voice, and wept; and they rent everyone his mantle, and sprinkled dust upon their heads toward heaven. So they sat down with him upon the ground seven days and seven nights, and none spake a word unto him: for they saw that *his* grief was very great.

His dear, friends come from far and wide to comfort him. Job 2:1 'Now when Job's three friends heard of all this evil that was come upon him, they came everyone from his own place; Eliphaz the Temanite, and Bildad the Shuhite, and Zophar the Namathite: for they made an appointment together to come and mourn with him and to comfort him.' Job's friends were like many of us, they did have good intentions. But just like us they just did not know the correct way to approach this unique situation. Can you find another account in the Bible of another man's troubles happening all at once as in Job's situation? Therefore this was unfamiliar territory for Job's friends. This is the same situation for us as ministers to the sick. Many times we also will go to visit someone and find we are in unfamiliar territory.

Job's friends did well at first, but when Job expressed his discomfort and grief they opened their mouths and said nothing comforting. They just made accusations by insinuating all Job's troubles were due to his lack of righteousness. Have you ever heard someone say that the person was ill because of something they did in their past? Or we said that drinking and smoking did them in? As a nurse I do know these things can be the root of diseases but only God knows the reason for allowing the sickness. We also need to be mindful when it is said the person is not praying enough or having enough faith. From the time of birth God has set up our journey. We can alter the path from His will but He also knows we will deter form the correct path. During difficult and trying times we as Christians tend to temporarily forget God has three answers to prayers; yes, not now and no.

You have most likely experienced this same situation regarding those in your family, friend circle or congregation that are sick or in mourning. For example, the mother who's newborn is born with a genetic problem or disability. The member who said she has been a non-smoker all her life that is now diagnosed with lung cancer. The Deacon diagnosed with AIDS. What do we as Christians need to do, to react, to serve and to minister to those in need?

As the community of faith believers we have an obligation to minister to this group. They need us more than ever. The government is not looking out for those who are sick. People are "kicked" out of hospitals as soon as they feel patients and/or family members can do the work themselves. As a home health nurse for a major medical university I am amazed at how many of my church members do not know all that is now done in the home and not the hospital. I see patients in the home that have intravenous medications such as fluids for dehydration, antibiotics for weeks up to months at a time. Many do chemotherapy at home. Extensive wound care is done by family members that 30 years ago was only done in the hospital. Patients go home with drains and tubes that must be cared for. Staples and stitches are removed in the home instead of the doctor's office. This is one reason I have spent so many years trying to serve those in need in the way that is beneficial to the recipient. Now that you know in general why this ministry is in demand let's begin by reviewing and learning some basics. We will also continue to rely on the guidance provided in the King James Version Bible. Each area explored will assist you in gleaning a better understanding of how to serve the body of Christ in need and how minister to the sick while also winning non-believers to Christ during times of crisis. I will discuss each area on order for you to glean a better understanding of how to serve the body of Christ in need as well as win the lost to Him. Everyone reading this has had situations surrounding these subjects and did not know what to do, or felt they said the wrong thing. The sadder situation is that they did not make a visit to the hospital, Skilled Nursing Facility or Hospice facility because of fears. As you think to yourself, I just cannot do that I want you to must remember two popular scriptures. The first is found in Philippians 4:13-14; I can do all things through Christ who strengthens me. Nevertheless you have done well that you shared in my distress. The second one is Deuteronomy 31:6; be strong and of a good courage, fear not, nor be afraid of them: for the LORD thy God, he *it is* that doth go with thee; he will not fail thee, nor forsake thee.

Other scriptures to encourage you follow:

Psalms 27: 1 The LORD *is* my light and my salvation; whom shall I fear? the LORD *is* the strength of my life; of whom shall I be afraid?

Isaiah 41:10 Fear thou not; for I *am* with thee: be not dismayed; for I *am* thy God: I will strengthen thee; yea, I will help thee; yea, I will uphold thee with the right hand of my righteousness.

Isaiah 41:13 For I the LORD thy God will hold thy right hand, saying unto thee, Fear not; I will help thee.

2 Timothy 1:7 For God hath not given us the spirit of fear; but of power, and of love, and of a sound mind.

These scriptures are also great for counseling to those who are afraid of the next steps or of the things unknown about their illness. Remember them as we discuss this later.

Chapter II

Illness a Season of Life Issue

There are many different types of illnesses. We can have a slight headache, a touch of headache, migraines or a headache that renders you unable to function at all. Each human being approaches illnesses differently. For the purpose of this study we need to define what we are talking about when it comes to ministering to those with chronic, severe or life threatening, and end of life illnesses.

Chronic vs. Life threatening Illness vs. "End of Life"

A chronic illness is an illness lasting a long time, persisting for 3 months or longer. A life threatening illness is one that if left untreated or is untreatable has the potential to be a cause of death. The End of Life is referred to as when a person's body is showing signs of actively dying.[27]

Impact of Illness

All of us have either been personally diagnosed with a serious illness, had a family member with one or visited a member of our congregation with a serious illness. It is rare to find someone who has not been affected by a serious illness personally or by their family or friends. All illnesses are a season of life issue. For many, illnesses are non-ending seasons of their lives.

In the 1900's the life expectancy was about 50 years, today it is 78 years with a growing number of persons living to the 90's and even over 100.[4] I am blessed to live in an area with three renowned hospital systems, Wake Medical, Duke Medical and UNC Health Care. Because of this, it is easy to see why people in the area where I live can feel like no one should be suffering. They assume everyone who presents with an illness can be easily treated and cured.

The illnesses that only a few years ago were considered death sentences are now not necessarily a death sentence. For example persons with AIDS, many cancers, liver diseases, and kidney diseases now live long and productive lives without pain and early deaths.

Nine out of ten persons in the U.S.A. will have a chronic or life threatening illness.[4] This is not a two – three day hospital stay, or just feeling bad for a day or two. These folks are ill; feeling poorly for weeks, months, years and decades.

As the faith community, the ministers of God, the believers of Christ it is important that we grasp what it means to live daily with these burdens so that we can be effective in our service to those in need.

What does the Bible instruct us to do and how to behave?

Romans 12:10 tells us to be kindly affectionate one to another with brotherly love, in honor preferring one another. Therefore we have an obligation to learn how to minister effectively to God's people in need.

1 Thessalonians 4:9; But as touching brotherly love ye need not that I write unto you: for ye yourselves are taught of God to love one another.

Hebrews 13:1-2; Let brotherly love continue. Be not forgetful to entertain strangers: for thereby some have entertained angels unawares.

1 Peter 3:8; Finally, *be ye* all of one mind, having compassion one of another, love as brethren, *be* pitiful, *be* courteous:

1 John 4:7-11 Beloved, let us love one another: for love is of God; and every one that loveth is born of God, and knoweth God. He that loveth not knoweth not God; for God is love.

In this was manifested the love of God toward us, because that God sent his only begotten Son into the world, that we might live through him. Herein is love, not that we loved God, but that he loved us, and sent his Son *to be* the propitiation for our sins. Beloved, if God so loved us, we ought also to love one another.

There is one more thing I want you to be aware of, persons with the same diagnosis or disease do not have the exact same symptoms or reactions. For example: At birth I was diagnosed with reactive airway disease but most people call it asthma because when I get in trouble or have a cold I will wheeze like an asthmatic. Reactive airway disease means I have many things I am allergic to. People with asthma are usually not allergic to anything that requires allergy shots or special allergy medication. Another fact to be aware of is that many people live with chronic or life threatening illnesses that do not require special care. They are able to work and live what appears to others as a normal life. When these persons are confined and now have progressed to a more serious phase of their illness even if it is temporary we need to treat them as if the diagnosis just happened.

Examples of Chronic/ Life Threatening Illnesses

- Dementia

- End Stage Liver

- Parkinson

- Heart Disease

- Diabetes

- End Stage Kidney

- Stroke

- Lung Diseases: COPD, Asthma, RAD

> Many people live with these that may not be in a condition that requires special care.

> Do not assume if someone seems to be OK that they do not need help.

This list is not all inclusive but it gives you an idea of the types of chronic/life threatening illnesses that someone may have.

No matter what the disease or serious illness, many who are affected experience changes in three basic areas. [3]

Areas of Impact:

*Physical   ***Emotional**   ***Spiritual**

Physical:

There are two areas that are affected in the physical. One is the activities of daily living that must continue to be done. The second is what happens to the functioning of the body.

What are activities of daily living? Things such as eating, sleeping, bathing, dressing, toileting, cooking, paying bills, making appointments, caring for children, going to work, driving, cleaning, getting medications, going to church, participating in clubs, recreation, all just a few of the broad categories of activities of daily living. When you think about these things can you now see more areas where we fail to minister? Have you considered this; the person who is ill was the driver for the household and now cannot drive? Did you think about this, person that is ill is the one who took care of the shopping, the budget scheduling appointments and the money? These things must be attended to. The faith community may not be able to do all of these things for the family and many times it is not appropriate for them to perform these duties. When assessing this area of ministry first find out who in the family has taken over some of these duties. Then look to see if friends or co-workers have pitched in to do some of the tasks. Then you are prepared to look at the tasks which have not been done and see which ones your ministry group can assist with. By following this guideline the person who is ill and family caring for them will be ministered to in a greater way. Remember these are beginning guidelines. The purpose of this writing is to begin the dialogue, start the education and open our eyes to areas where we have not done all that could be done by the faith community.

Now let's look at the area of what the illness can do to the body. We will start with pain. The Oxford English Dictionary defines pain as three distinct types:

- Physical Suffering or discomfort caused by illness or injury
- Mental suffering or distress
- An annoying or tedious person or thing, or object.[24]

There are two categories of pain; acute and chronic pain. WebMD states acute pain is sudden onset of pain.[25] Treatments for acute pain usually focus on treating the condition that has caused the pain. Medical professionals define chronic pain as pain that has lasted for six months or more and disrupts work, play, sleep, family life, emotions and faith.

One out of three people suffers from chronic pain. Chronic pain is pain that has lasted longer than the expected length of time.[25] It can result from injury or disease, or it may have no known cause or reason. In contrast, acute pain comes on suddenly and can serve as the body's warning signal that something may be wrong or it comes as a result of surgery or injury. Have you been to visit or minister to someone in pain? It can be very difficult to visit, comfort and minister to someone in pain. It can make the person with the strongest of faith and emotional stability shaky. Those who minister to someone in pain can experience a feeling of helplessness. What can you do? Always acknowledge the pain. Pain is real. Pain is different, subjective for each person. One person's headache is not the same as another person's headache. Even if the doctors do not know why a person has pain, it is real.

About 16 years ago I had a severe sharp pain at my belly button after eating. My regular doctor could not find any reason as to why I would hurt where my pain was located. He gave me the name of a specialist and told me to make an appointment. He did express that he did believe I had pain. But he also stated he did not know what the problem could be. The only thing to do was to put me to sleep and do some tests. After the tests were completed he reported I had several very large colon polyps that he removed and sent to pathology while I was asleep. He explained the pathology report revealed these were the type that that research shows would have become cancerous if not removed in a timely fashion. The doctor then stated that it was a blessing that I had the pain which resulted in getting the tests down. Then he proceeded to tell me that he still could not understand how I had pain where I did because there are no nerve endings in that area that could trigger pain. He said God was looking out for me. And of course I agreed with the doctor and told him; yes, God always does look out for me!

What was helpful in how I was treated? Both doctors believed me when I said I had pain, even though they both knew it was not a place most people would have pain. Both admitted they did not have the answers, but they wanted to assist me in getting relief. Once the cause and remedy was identified the doctor promptly explained what was going on and the plan from there.

So what can we do? Acknowledge that you believe they have pain. I have heard well meaning visitors tell a person with severe pain after surgery to deal with it and that they do not want to get hooked on the medicine. Or just pray to stop the pain, it does not hurt that much. Or the worst of all;

I did not have pain when I had surgery. Why are these statements unhelpful and not portraying the love of Jesus? Let's go back to the previous statements: **Pain is real. Pain is different, subjective for each person. One person's headache is not the same as another person's headache. Even if the doctors do not know why a person has pain, it is real.**

Assist those in pain by telling them to never apologize for having pain. Reassure them it is real but they can control it and not let it control them. They will need to do things differently but you will continue to minister to them. William S. Halsey said, "All the problems become smaller if you don't dodge them, but confront them. Touch a thistle timidly, and it pricks you; grasp it boldly, and its spine crumbles."

What can you do or say as you minister or counsel those in pain? Pray with them if they are able, if not pray for them. Let them understand it is okay to ask for medication if they need it. It is not a sign of spiritual weakness by taking medication as it was designed by God when he allowed man to make it. There are many alternate therapies that are helpful depending on the type and reason for the pain. For example after a muscle or bone surgery or injury; ice or cold therapy is very soothing. It is usually limited to 10-15 minutes at a time but the doctors can direct and order this. For some pain heat therapy is helpful. This can also be ordered by the physician as to the time and duration and frequency. The one method not used as much as we should is distraction therapy. Distraction therapy uses anything that will have the person concentrate on something beside the pain.[25] Some examples are listening to soothing music, watching a favorite movie or video of a favorite place. Also talking about a happy event, concentrating on a puzzle, reading a book that is interesting can be used as distraction therapy. For children playing with a favorite toy or a favorite game can be distracting therapy. Encourage the person to talk to their family and caregivers about pain and pain control needs. Acknowledge that you believe them when they have a complaint of pain. For example say, "You said you are hurting? Where is your pain?" Ask them what helped the last time to them get through the pain or to ease it off. Do as they ask, if possible and then start to minister, some will like prayer, some just want you to hold their hand. Others like for you to rub the area, or to just sit and be quiet. Some just want you to be there quietly praying while they go through the pain. If they say they just do not know what to do you can always pray for them. If they do not want any noise, pray silently as God eases the pain. If the person says I am okay, believe it and stay, do not leave right then. Give them a while, pray silently, until they are ready for you to talk etc.

What if they say they are worried they will have pain for the rest of their life? Counsel them to just get through this moment. This will help by taking their mind off the uncertain future and decrease the anxiety thinking about a difficult future brings.

Assist the person in pain to get closer to God. Many times a formerly devote Christian can blame God or wonder why He has allowed this suffering. Remember these passages of scripture:

2 Corinthians 1: 3-5 Blessed *be* God, even the Father of our Lord Jesus Christ, the Father of mercies, and the God of all comfort; Who comforteth us in all our tribulation, that we may be able to comfort them which are in any trouble, by the comfort wherewith we ourselves are comforted of God. For as the sufferings of Christ abound in us, so our consolation also aboundeth by Christ.

Luke 8:46-48 And Jesus said, Somebody hath touched me: for I perceive that virtue is gone out of me. And when the woman saw that she was not hid, she came trembling, and falling down before him, she declared unto him before all the people for what cause she had touched him, and how she was healed immediately. And he said unto her, Daughter, be of good comfort: thy faith hath made thee whole; go in peace.

Psalm 23: 4 Yea, though I walk through the valley of the shadow of death, I will fear no evil: for thou *art* with me; thy rod and thy staff they comfort me.

Psalm 71: 17-21 O God, thou hast taught me from my youth: and hitherto have I declared thy wondrous works. Now also when I am old and greyheaded, O God, forsake me not; until I have showed thy strength unto *this* generation, *and* thy power to every one *that* is to come.

Thy righteousness also, O God, *is* very high, who hast done great things: O God, who *is* like unto thee! *Thou*, which hast showed me great and sore troubles, shalt quicken me again, and shalt bring me up again from the depths of the earth.

Thou shalt increase my greatness, and comfort me on every side. For those who do not know Jesus as savior this may be the time to introduce the loving and comfort of salvation during a person's painful times.[1] Here are a few scriptures that will guide them to know who takes all pain away. Use others as you wish:

John 3:16 For God so loved the world, that he gave his only begotten Son, that whosoever believeth in him should not perish, but have everlasting life.

John 14:16-18 And I will pray the Father, and he shall give you another Comforter, that he may abide with you for ever; *Even* the Spirit of truth; whom the world cannot receive, because it seeth him not, neither knoweth him: but ye know him; for he dwelleth with you, and shall be in you. I will not leave you comfortless: I will come to you.

Romans 1:16 For I am not ashamed of the gospel of Christ: for it is the power of God unto salvation to every one that believeth; to the Jew first, and also to the Greek.

Romans 10:10-13 For with the heart man believeth unto righteousness; and with the mouth confession is made unto salvation. For the scripture saith, Whosoever believeth on him shall not be ashamed. For there is no difference between the Jew and the Greek: for the same Lord over all is rich unto all that call upon him. For whosoever shall call upon the name of the Lord shall be saved.

Psalm 119: 73-77 Thy hands have made me and fashioned me: give me understanding, that I may learn thy commandments. They that fear thee will be glad when they see me; because I have hoped in thy word. I know, O LORD, that thy judgments *are* right, and *that* thou in faithfulness hast afflicted me. Let, I pray thee, thy merciful kindness be for my comfort, according to thy word unto thy servant. Let thy tender mercies come unto me, that I may live: for thy law *is* my delight.

Psalm 119: 81-82. My soul fainteth for thy salvation: *but* I hope in thy word. Mine eyes fail for thy word, saying, When wilt thou comfort me?

Revelation 21: 4 And God shall wipe away all tears from their eyes; and there shall be no more death, neither sorrow, nor crying, neither shall there be any more pain: for the former things are passed away.

You would be surprised how sometimes having a person who just listens and understands without judgment will help the discomfort.

What if they ask for medications is this okay? Do not let your personal feelings over take your opinions. The Bible states in 2 Corinthians 12:9, My grace is sufficient for thee: for my strength is made perfect in weakness. Matthew Henry in his Commentary on the New Testament states "My grace is sufficient for thee. Though God accepts the prayer of faith, yet he does not always answer it in the letter; as he sometimes grants in wrath, so he sometimes denies in love. When God does not remove our troubles and temptations, yet, if he gives us grace sufficient for us, we have no reason to complain, nor to say that he deals ill by us. It is a great comfort to us, whatever thorns in the flesh we are pained with, that God's grace is sufficient for us.[2] Grace signifies two things:

[1.] The good-will of God towards us and this is enough to enlighten and enliven us, sufficient to strengthen and comfort us, to support our souls and cheer up our spirits, in all afflictions and distresses.

[2.] The good work of God in us, the grace we receive from the fullness that is in Christ our head; and from him there shall be communicated that which is suitable and seasonable, and sufficient for his members. Christ Jesus understands our case, and knows our need, and will proportion the remedy to our malady, and not only strengthen us, but glorify himself. His strength is made perfect in our weakness.[1]

This does not say medications are not to be taken when needed. All things that God made are good when used for His glory. He does not want us to suffer.

There is a Pain Care Bill of Rights. It was established by the American Pain Foundation to assure that patients that are in pain due to illness, or medical procedures are not ignored or allowed to suffer.

Pain Care Bill of Rights:

People with pain have the right to:

- Have the report of pain taken seriously and to be treated with dignity and respect by doctors, nurses, pharmacists and other health professionals

- Have their pain thoroughly assessed and promptly treated

- Be informed by their doctors about what may be causing the pain, possible treatments, and the benefits, risks and costs of each.

- Participate actively in decisions about how to manage the pain

- Have the pain reassessed regularly and the treatment adjusted if the pain has not eased

- Be referred to a pain specialist if the pain persists and

- Get clear and prompt answers to their questions, have time to make decisions and refuse a particular type of treatment if they choose. [3]

Mental suffering or distress pain

This area of pain is frequently over looked by everyone except the medical community. The losses of control of day to day life can be very hard on many persons. Many people can hide their feelings from others but the stress will come out in other ways. Anger towards the person who is doing the majority of the care giving is common. It is okay to ask, tell me how you are dealing with being confined? What can I do to make it easier for you? Or you can ask how are handling this being that you have always taken care of everyone else? Follow with; how you are doing having everyone else do for you? This helps to open the door for a conversation about areas that need to be addressed and ministered. Help others working with the ill person understand what is going on. And do not forget; pray for and with them both.

An annoying or tedious person or thing, or object.

The clergy always have to deal with the annoying or energy sapping person. Some have a unique way to limit the amount of time they must spend at each encounter with the person. Others get caught in the web and feel trapped waiting for a rescuer to show up. This is the same with a person who is relying on another person to take care of them that is driving them crazy. It does not matter if you and others on the outside feel there is no problem. Watch the interaction between those in the home. The stress and worries of the illness can exhibit itself in many ways. Prayer, understanding without judgment, and helping by just being around is needed. The annoying thing or object during a serious illness can be repeated tests, a tube in your body, a ostomy wound or any other frequent unwanted change to your pervious self.

Emotional:

Wendy Wallace a devote Christian and author has twenty four severe illnesses, four of which are considered life threatening. In her book 'Doing Well at Being Sick', she notes that it is difficult for anyone who is ill to accept that they have a serious or life threatening illness that affects their lives. She says the first barrier for her was her irrational self confidence, and independence. She also wrote she decided if she did not talk or think about it then the illness did not exist. [5]

When faced with a serious illness or life threatening diagnosis disbelief can occur, not the kind that comes from our belief in the Master's hand on our lives, but the kind that can result in bad outcomes. For example: a man is hospitalized in a coma, his blood sugar is over 1000, when he awakes the doctors tell him it is a miracle he is alive. They explain he has diabetes. He says I don't have diabetes

I just ate too much sugar yesterday. He continues to eat incorrectly and not take the insulin prescribed and ends up back in the hospital in a diabetic coma.

As ministers we need to help people accept the state they are in now as a season of their life. Using God's words to let them know this is happening now and we will ask God for guidance in dealing with this change. Remind them they are not alone. The faith community is always saying God is with you but during this type of situation people need humans with them. Just don't leave without assuring there will be someone around. If the person does not want anyone around them try using technology by calling, e-mailing, sending cards etc. to let them know and feel the love of God.

Other emotional states that may occur when faced with serious illness or life threatening diagnosis are anxiety, grief, and depression.

Anxiety is a feeling of worry, nervousness, or unease about something with an uncertain outcome.[24] A change in health can involve new tests, new words, many doctors, nurses and other health personnel. There can be too much to understand and retain. The unknown brings fear.

A friend of mine had been given a diagnosis of colon cancer. She became so nervous about the surgery the doctors recommended that she could decide not to have the surgery. The tumor continued to grown causing her much pain. As her friend, I noticed her uneasiness and was able to minister to and pray with and for her. This gave her the assistance to relieve her anxiety. She could then make the decisions regarding her treatment. .

Grief is normally thought of as what happens when someone dies. We will discuss this in later chapters. This type of grief brings intense sorrow, trouble or annoyance about the things that have or may change forever. For example, the loss of hair during chemotherapy, the loss of appetite, and loss of the ability to do things for yourself can cause a person to grieve over what was. I am sure you can now think of other situations that could cause grief for someone who has a serious illness. The signs that someone is grieving about a serious illness or life threatening diagnosis are many. Some common ones are rejecting treatment plans, missing medical appointments, and isolation from social activities. The following except from a well known hymn sums it all up beautifully.

"Trust and Obey"

Not a burden we bear, Not a sorrow we share,

But our toil he doth richly repay, Not a grief nor a loss,

Not a frown or a cross, But is blest if we trust and obey.[4]

Depression is one of the most common unnoticed symptoms of serious illness or life threatening diagnosis. It is normal to be sad, but depression is not normal. Grieving over the changes that have or will occur as a result of the serious or life threatening illness is to be expected. Clinical depression can cause impaired functioning and distress, an inability to make treatment decisions or any decisions. When a person is clinically depressed our role as ministers to those with serious illness or life threatening diagnosis is to observe and identify the indications that the person is not just sad but now in need of intervention.

The following illustrates the signs of depression that you need to be aware of.

A Closer Look at Depression - Common symptoms of depression:

❖ Loss of interest or pleasure in daily activities that previously gave pleasure.

- ❖ Significant weight loss or weight gain.

- ❖ Sleeping too, much or too, little.

- ❖ Unable to concentrate, distracted.

- ❖ Lack of feeling or emotion.

- ❖ Feeling of worthlessness or guilt.

- ❖ Fatigue, loss of energy.

- ❖ Repeated thoughts or verbalizations about death or suicide.

- ❖ Hopelessness

- ❖ Inability or trouble making decisions, or remembering important things[3]

As ministers to those in need we cannot ignore the above signs when we see them. Many times a family member and medical personnel assume the signs they see are related to the shock of the news or the treatment they are giving. The use of prayer and discernment will assist in indentifying when help with depression is necessary. The standard definition used by medical personnel for clinical depression is the presence of five or more of the symptoms listed above nearly on a daily basis for two or more weeks.[26] This may indicate a need for a professional assistance with depression. If you notice the symptoms are increasing and not resolving it is your obligation to notify the family of the need for medical attention, by describing what you see. Many times just listening, praying, companionship, or allowing the person to vent is all that is needed to lift the spirits of someone who does not have the signs of clinical depression.

Spiritual:

This area is one that ministers of faith say they are comfortable with. What about when a formerly devoted Christian has lost their way? Suffering persons often experience what they think is God's lack of response to their prayers for a cure or relief. Your loving presence and prayer may help them realize God's love again.[26] Many people with life threatening illnesses do feel isolated from God. They may feel God has left them. The ministers can be like robots sometimes giving canned responses without letting the person get it all out in the open. This can be uncomfortable for you but it is important for the healing of the soul. It is easy to accept the joyful directions God's plan for our life takes us. But it can be very difficult to accept and understand the valley seasons of our life. Reminders from the Bible are needed but only after the burdens have been shared. Then remind them of the words in:

Romans 8: 26-28 Likewise the Spirit also helpeth our infirmities: for we know not what we should pray for as we ought: but the Spirit itself maketh intercession for us with groanings which cannot be uttered. And he that searcheth the hearts knoweth what *is* the mind of the Spirit, because he maketh intercession for the saints according to *the will of* God. And we know that all things work together for good to them that love God, to them who are the called according to *his* purpose.

When we pray sincerely to God we confess our dependence on Him. God gives us light to apply to the dark problems and situations of our lives. But how about when you have to minister to an unsaved family member of a saved person? Find out where they stand on the subject of God, Jesus and salvation. This conversation may be harsh with language that is not pleasant. The reason for this conversation is to understand what has not been working or what was rejected. Pray for direction and discernment to hear between the words that are spoken or better yet the words that are left unspoken. Our primary obligation is to start delivering the message of salvation in a way the person has never heard before. No lectures or 'preaching'. Kind gentle words of the glory of salvation and the simplicity of becoming a Christian in the simple terms will win a soul to Christ quicker than ultimatums or force. Conveying the love of the master and the joy of salvation is the key to opening the door. Effective ministers of God's Kingdom should not be identified by the badge on their lapel, or the introduction with their title, but by the manner and words of God's love that ooze all around them.

Once they are ready to hear about salvation the easy part is repeating the scriptures that guide us all to salvation.

John 3:16-17 For God so loved the world, that he gave his only begotten Son, that whosoever believeth in him should not perish, but have everlasting life. For God sent not his Son into the world to condemn the world; but that the world through him might be saved.

Romans10:9-10 ...that if you confess with your mouth the lord Jesus and believe in your heart that God has raised Him from the dead, you will be saved. For with the heart one believes unto righteousness, and with the mouth confession is made unto salvation.

When you have to Minister to someone who says God has forgotten all about me.

Or they say, He does not care about me and my problems any more. Remember these scriptures and add your own.

Hebrews 13:5b for he hath said I will never leave thee nor forsaken thee.

Jeremiah 29:11-12 For I know the thoughts that I think toward you, saith the LORD, thoughts of peace, and not of evil, to give you an expected end. Then shall ye call upon me, and ye shall go and pray unto me, and I will hearken unto you.

Jeremiah 29:11-12 NKJV; For I know the plans I have for you , Declares the Lord, plans for welfare and not for calamity to give you a future and a hope. Then you will call upon Me and come and pray to Me, and I will listen to you.

Psalms 37: 25 I have been young, and now am old; yet have I not seen the righteous forsaken, nor his seed begging bread.

Remind them of the power of praise, and prayer. Increase your time and companionship. Rally others to fill in the gaps of visitation and companionship. Make visits without rushing to go to the next place.

What if they say things that let you know they have lost faith and feel separated from God?

Romans 8:38-39 For I am persuaded that neither death nor life, nor angels nor principalities nor powers, nor things present nor things to come , nor height nor depth, nor any other created thing, shall be able to separate us from the love of God which is in Jesus Christ.

What if a confession of hidden sins from someone who you thought or know is saved? What if they are not saved?

Romans 3;23 For all have sinned, and come short of the glory of God;

Romans 5: 12-16 Wherefore, as by one man sin entered into the world, and death by sin; and so death passed upon all men, for that all have sinned: (For until the law sin was in the world: but sin is not imputed when there is no law. Nevertheless death reigned from Adam to Moses, even over them that had not sinned after the similitude of Adam's transgression, who is the figure of him that was to come. But not as the offence, so also *is* the free gift. For if through the offence of one many be dead, much more the grace of God, and the gift by grace, *which is* by one man, Jesus Christ, hath abounded unto many. And not as *it was* by one that sinned, *so is* the gift: for the judgment *was* by one to condemnation, but the free gift *is* of many offences unto justification.

John 3:16-18 For God so loved the world that he gave his only begotten Son, that whosoever believeth in him should not perish but have everlasting life. For God sent not his Son into the world to condemn the world; but that the world through him might be saved.

He that believeth on him is not condemned: but he that believeth not is condemned already, because he hath not believed in the name of the only begotten Son of God.

What about lack of support from the faith community?

Many of us feel we have done our part when we do the weekly Sunday afternoon visitation call. We put the names on the prayer list. We stay thirty minutes or so, smile, sing a song, pray and maybe give communion. There is nothing wrong with this practice. The problem is this; when a person has a serious illness or life threatening disease there needs to be more than a weekly visit. Just like we need more than a once a week prayer and praise session we need to minister to those with severe illnesses more than one time a week. I can hear what you must be thinking. Sometimes they act like they do not want me to come. Call and make an effort. Many times they just don't feel you want to be there. You are awful busy and always rushing to and fro. Or they may not feel well when you arrive unannounced. The pastor should not be the only one visiting. Every member who is a born again believer can be a part of the visiting team.

2 Samuel 12: 19-23 But when David saw that his servants whispered, David perceived that the child was dead:

therefore David said unto his servants, Is the child dead? And they said, He is dead. The David arose from the earth, and washed, and anointed himself, and changed his apparel, and came into the house of the Lord, and worshipped; then he came to his own house; and when he required, they set bread before him and he did eat. Then said his servants unto him, What thing is this that thou hast done? Didst fast and weep for the child, while it was alive; but when the child was dead thou didst rise and eat bread. And he said, While the child was yet alive I fasted and wept: for I said, Who can tell whether God will be gracious to me , that the child may live? But now he is dead, therefore should I fast? can I bring him back again? I shall go to him, but he shall not return to me.

Growth Opportunities During Illness

It is hard to imagine that there could be growth of any kind during a chronic or life threatening illness. There are two areas of growth that we will discuss; Power and Education.

Power

Those with serious illness do have power they can tap into especially those who are saved. Also many will seek knowledge obtained through education during these times.

- ❖ The Power to Grow in Faith: develop new ministries, create and start new ventures, complete thing they never could do before.

- ❖ The Power to Receive: receive needed services, and assistance that may have been rejected in the past. Becoming open to asking others for the help they need.

- ❖ The Power to Give: by assisting with giving hope to others with the same or other illnesses, giving wisdom to their friends and family.

❖ The Power to Advocate: speaking up to get the best medical care, to ask questions to understand medical terms and issues, to assure desired wishes are cared out, make personalized decisions about your health and care

❖ The Power to Lead: a change in prospective, beliefs and quality of life[3]

The Power to Grow in Faith

Elizabeth Edwards, a prominent figure in the political world, was at the end stages of terminal cancer. She created a gift to her small children of individual journals. These journals contained the wisdom she wanted to teach each one of her children.[28]

The Power to Receive

One of the most difficult areas for many with serious illnesses and disability is asking for help. How many times have we called someone one on our sick and shut in list and said, "If there is anything I can do just let me know? We all say this or something similar. But what is wrong with statements like this? Many times the person is too busy thinking about the things of getting well or others issues to even know what they need. The burden of having to call someone to ask for things is just another thing to put on their long list. The more useful approach is to just think about things we all use each day. Toilet paper, paper towels, bottle water, tissues, all of these items are helpful to any person going through illnesses. Call and say instead, I am coming to see you at 1 p.m., do you have a special brand of toilet paper you use. See how much easier it would be to accept this assistance. You may even get a focused reply such as I have enough toilet paper but I don't think I have any paper towels. This really will open up the conversation. If the person really does not open up go make the visit and be observant as to what is needed. Don't be in a hurry when you arrive. Wait until you can visit when you will not appear rushed. It is not easy to ask for assistance when it appears the person that could help is in a hurry and would not have the time to complete the task.

I have always been the one who cared for others. When I have been ill with pneumonia or severe reactive airway disease, I would decline any offered assistance from friends or family. I would give the "I'm okay, I have what I need" speech. Even when I broke my foot and could not drive I received a call from my church family stating they were coming to do my chores. I again used my familiar response, "I'm okay, you don't have to do this" But this time my Pastor responded with, "We are on our way, do not get up and hurt yourself." Of course I tried and they caught me, but I was given an appropriate lecture on acceptance of help. Years later when I had my knee replaced no one heard the old "I'm okay" speech, I responded thank you, I will be glad to see you. I developed the power to receive during this illness.

Here is another example from one who lives to help, myself, but has a very hard time receiving help; however I was fortunate to have some church members that ministered to me correctly. It was a rainy afternoon and on my way to see a burn patient, I fell down going to the car. I heard a snap of my left foot and left knee. Praying to God to help me get up from the pavement, I got in my manual transmission car. I then drove two miles to my patient's house and changed the dressings to his burns. This took about one hour. At the end of the visit we both realized I had really hurt myself. I promised him I would go to get my foot checked out. I used my left foot to push the clutch and drove the one mile to the orthopedic doctor's office. My left foot was broken and my left knee was severely sprained. I called one of my fellow church members to tell her I would not be at choir practice, because I had fallen and fractured my foot. She asked how was I getting home, and how was I going to get my car home. I was in Durham and I live in Chatham County which is twenty miles apart. I informed her that my supervisor was coming to take me home but I had not even thought about my car being left at the medical office. She said her daughter will ride with her to choir practice. They will leave the church then come to my house to get the car keys. She would then take her daughter to get my car and follow her back to my house and leave my car and then go home. She did not give me a chance to say a word she spoke in the soft sweet voice of power and reason becoming the angel of rescue that I needed when I did not even know I needed her. All I could do is say thank you many times, with her reply of do not to worry about it. This is how we need to minister to those who need to develop the power to receive.

The Power to Give

In the early 1950's there was no cure or treatments for most cancers. My father was diagnosed with prostate cancer before my two sisters and I were born. My father knew the likelihood of his living to see us become adults was slim based on the information the medical professionals gave him. Therefore he used every minute of what was to be his last 13 years teaching my sisters and me the things he felt were important in order for us to become productive, educated, beloved women. He wanted us to become women who would make a difference in this world. I thank God for putting these teachings upon his heart.

Elizabeth Edwards was a loving mother that realized when her cancer was back she may not live to see her children grow up. She knew what she saw in each one of them and the things she wanted them to know from her and the things she believed. To accomplish this she left each one herself. Elizabeth Edwards's gift to her small children was individual customized journals of the wisdom she wanted to teach each one.[28]

I had a patient that I provided hospice services to. Prior to her illness she was a hard working Christian. Each year on resurrection Sunday she gave out white crocheted crosses to everyone in her church. She then went visiting those who were in the hospital, nursing homes and confined to home passing out the rest of her "Resurrection Day" crosses. She lit up with joy telling me how she was able to tell the story of Jesus this way. She felt she would not see the next Resurrection Sunday. So in the fall she started making the crosses. The difference was she made them red. I still have the one she gave me on what turned out to be my last visit.

She ended this life just before Christmas that year. But every nurse, doctor, and medical person that came to her room and could not tell her the salvation story received the way to salvation from her. After her death her daughter told me she made enough of her red Resurrection Day crosses to be given to her church family at Christmas. This is a powerful gift she left for her friends, family and the persons who needed the gift of salvation.[20]

The Power to Advocate

The Oxford Dictionary defines advocate as a person who pleads a case on someone else's behalf, a person who publicly supports or recommends a particular cause.[24] Our advocate is Jesus Christ. He should be our example whenever we advocate for those in need. Our duty when caring for the sick is to convey that their faith and the strength it can bring, is a powerful resource in the times of suffering. God has promised to remain steadfast during our trials and tribulation.

1Samuel 12:22 For the LORD will not forsake his people for his great name's sake: because it hath pleased the LORD to make you his people.

1 Corinthians 15:58 Therefore, my beloved brethren, be ye steadfast, unmoveable, always abounding in the work of the Lord, forasmuch as ye know that your labour is not in vain in the Lord.

How can we be an advocate beyond prayer? How can we portray the love of Jesus into the everyday things that must be done during an illness?

Have you seen the commercial where the girl is in the restaurant and asks her waiter so many questions he cannot even answer the first question? In the next scene she is sitting at the doctor's office. The doctor asks her if she had any questions or concerns and she doesn't even open her mouth. She shakes her head no, and shrugs her shoulders. Have you ever felt this way at the doctor's office? I have. I remember when I was sitting in the doctor's office to find out the results of a cat scan to see what was causing me to bleed so much as I was severely anemic.

The doctor comes in with his stiffly starched white coat. Sits down with a somber face that I have never seen before and tells me the scan indicated I had multiple tumors and there was a high probability they were cancerous. He continued to talk, I know because I saw his mouth moving but I only heard: "jdkshau iofheuwqrfhuf bffiwebf qwhfuebf webfq." He then asked any questions about the surgery? I sat there like a deaf mute. Finally I said what? He then said you understand what I said right, you are a registered nurse right? I finally said Doctor, right now I am not a nurse I am the patient, now start over and go over what you said after the word cancer.

He apologized and did let me know what was going on in simple everyday terms. But I knew then why everyone can use an advocate.

It is very intimidating to speak up at the doctor's office for many people especially when you are sick and you don't want poor care. As in the above story many doctors do not mean to be insensitive. They just do not give you the time to process each step before going on to the next. It is helpful if someone is there with you. Not to watch your exam but to help with the instructions and relay information that may be over looked. This role of minister advocates is one we must be willing to fulfill when appropriate. Now of course you don't take over. Not even if it is your spouse or other family member. You are there to fill in the gaps, to write down the details for recall later.

You are the buffer for nervous lack of memory and the human rock to lean on as prayers are being uttered as you wait for test results to be revealed. You are not there to react to the information. The person may need your "Joy of the Lord" as they gather their strength. Of course if the news is one for praising and rejoicing let them guide you as how much to say or do.

After the surgery I did not find out if the tumors were cancerous or not for about three weeks. The longest three weeks I can remember. I did not even tell my sisters what was on my heart. I burdened God with this need. The day I was to find out the outcome of the pathology of the tumors, I had a very close friend drive me to the doctor. When my name was called I asked her to go in the room with me. She had no idea why I asked her to come in because I had not told her about my greatest fears. After all I was only 32 years old. When the doctor walked in with a great big smile on his face I knew it had to be good news. He handed me the report and all I read was "but no cancer cells found". I threw the chart down and started giving thanks to God. My friend did not know what I was thanking God for but she joined in. When we calmed down the doctor explained all the details. My friend started crying for joy over God's healing mercies over me. Later she did fuss about me not telling her but she understood I did not want her worried about me.

Whether you assist someone to speak up to get their needs met or the treatment they prefer, learning to minister as an advocate can assist the person to be empowered to be their own advocate.[2] We need to educate those who are ill, their family members and loved ones that the health care community expects patients and families to assert themselves when it comes to their health care needs. They want to know if the medication they gave you is too, expensive. How can they offer an alternative or enroll you in a free medication program if you do not tell them. A doctor friend of mine told me a long time ago that the field of medicine is full of unanswered questions. Many times the doctor is really just making the best guess based on what information the patient gives them, whether verbally or what is found on the exam. So it is the best thing to give as much information as possible to help your doctor win the guessing game.

Being a nurse I like to watch medical shows. There is one that deals with the difficult to diagnose illnesses. One of the episodes was about a woman who came in with complains of severe itching. She told the doctor she thought she ate something that she was allergic to. So he treated her for an allergic reaction. She got better. About two weeks later she had a headache and flu symptoms. They treated her for the flu. She then passed out while telling her friend she thought there were mice or rats in the house she was renting because she heard scratching noises in the kitchen. She was rushed to the hospital and the friend told them everything except about the rats she thought was in the home. She got better and the landlord called an exterminator to come. A raccoon was found in her kitchen. They said they got him and she should not hear anymore scratching sounds. She then ended up in the hospital very ill and went into a coma. Her friend then was determined to see what was going on and had the home inspected by a service that specialized in raccoon and wild animal removal. They found over 45 adult raccoons hidden in her home and many babies. He informed her to tell the doctors to start treatment for the mites that they carry. After the treatment she recovered and moved in with her girlfriend.

Sometimes the fear of saying or doing the wrong thing keeps us from being the advocate to someone facing a serious illness. It is also difficult to advocate for someone who has been ill for a long time. It can begin to seem like you are a bother or a nuisance. The feeling of will you make things worse can surface also.

As a home health registered nurse I have seen this situation happen to many previously strong monarchs of the family that are now patients and caregivers going through the trials of serious illnesses. One recent lady was always the rock of her family. A Christian with strong faith she became sick and assumed it was just a stomach virus or flu. Unfortunately she became so ill that she had to be transported to the hospital by ambulance. She was soon diagnosed with cancer. Surgery was offered as a treatment followed by radiation and chemotherapy both to be given each day.

Due to the shock and fear of the poor prognosis the patient agreed to the surgery. Two of her daughters did not want her to go through all of this, but they had not developed the power of advocacy yet. After seeing their mother get weaker and weaker and her vision in her right eye decrease to where she could not read or see objects on the right side, the power of advocacy grew within the two daughters. They started asking me questions, about her treatments and her functions. They asked their mother in my presence what she thought about continuing therapy. They asked that I notify the medical team in writing about the concerns they wished to discuss with them prior to receiving her next treatment. This way the medical team would not prepare chemo medication that they may decide not to take. With a small amount of coaching, the daughters were able to approach the medical team at their mother's next visit to convey her wishes. [20]

As ministers we need to act as sounding boards for people to talk to. We cannot convey our personal opinions or feelings. We cannot state what we would do or what we did or what someone we know did. Each person is different. Each disease is different. God gives us all the right to make our own decisions. We need to guide those who are having a difficult time being an advocate by using the courage God gives us through His Holy Spirit. Listen, listen and then listen some more, to the concerns they have about being an advocate. Help them discuss with other family members that are not saved in understanding the next steps Christians make. Or if they are saved and the person who is ill is not saved, help them in approaching their loved one with love and kindness as talk to them about the way to salvation.

Remember when we ask God to lead us sit quietly and wait on Him, he will direct our path. Assist the person who is sick and the caregivers to obtain as much information about the decisions they face. Guide them to the persons, the social worker or the nurse manager for their physician, who can help them. The following is a situation that may occur that is helpful in practicing how to deal with difficult situations. After you go over it reflect on some situations that have happened to you and talk them out with other members of the church who minister to the sick.

Example: Dr. Jones asks your friend Sis. Jane: Are the pain medicines giving you a sick stomach? Sis Jane says, no. You know this is not true. So, try saying in a sweet quiet voice, something like, Sis Jane, remember yesterday you were so sick you told me you thought you would not keep your lunch down. Then Sis Jane may feel comfortable enough to say, Oh yeah I did, I forgot about it. Remember you can comfort her by saying, you soon went to sleep and felt better later on, I don't think I would remember this small detail if I had gone to sleep. This will make her feel less anxious about forgetting this detail or being afraid to say something.

Following is the Keys to Patient Advocacy, developed by Tiffany Christensen, diagnosed with Cystic Fibrosis, a genetic disease of the lungs. You can find out more about her journey and work with patient advocacy in her book Sick Girl Speaks: Lessons and Ponderings Along the Road to Acceptance.[10] She developed this tools from the vantage point of a patient.

Three Keys to Patient Advocacy

1. Knowledge

❖ Access the internet: Medical technical sites for those who want very detailed and advanced information as well as general information sites written in simple terms are available via the internet. Use caution and understand there are a lot of incorrect information sites. Asking medical professionals for sites they would recommend is a great way to start.

It is important that you go to web sites that are credible. For example, for the diagnosis of cancer the following sites are deemed by the medical profession as being sites they encourage patients and family to go to:

- American Cancer Society

    www.cancer.org

- Cancer.Net

    www.cancer.net/portal/site/patient

- National Cancer Institute

    www.cancer.gov

- Cancer Network

    www.nccn.org

For information on other diseases and medications these sites are very helpful:

- Centers for Disease Control & Prevention (CDC) www.cdc.gov

- National Institutes of Health (NIH) www.nih.gov

- Web-MD www.webmd.com

- U.S. Food and Drug Administration (FDA) www.fda.gov/health/providers

❖ Ask questions: There is only one dumb question the one you do not ask. Do not worry about how to pronounce the medical terms. Use the words you know to describe what you need and keep asking until you understand. Ask for a different person to explain. Write your questions down and have a friend ask for you or have them read by the person who is answering them. Never be afraid to just ask.

❖ Talk with other persons who are going through similar situations. Ask the medical personnel about support groups or classes. The doctor or his nurse or the social worker for the team of doctors will now of support groups or others that are going through your treatment. They can also connect you with those who have recovered or learned to live with the illness or condition you have.

❖ Keep records of medications and treatments that you have had, have the "simple" names written beside the procedures for ease of understanding. Record which treatments or which medications were helpful. This can serve as a valuable guide for your health professionals in giving you the best care and developing a treatment plan that works for you.

2. Awareness

When sick, we all just want to close our eyes and let the medical folk just take care of us. Being aware of what is being given and when can make the difference of life and death. If you are too ill or unable to monitor and write down the details have someone with you who can do this. Be aware of the treatments and medication being given to you. Have a written list of allergies or adverse reactions to medications with you at all time. Mistakes are made by good intentioned medical personnel. Being alert and aware or having an advocate to do this may save your life.

3. Boundaries

When you do not understand what is being done or why it is being done do not be afraid to say, "Wait a minute." Ask for clarification and if you are still not satisfied ask to speak to your medical doctor. Now always do this in a humble, polite, Christian manner, but be the selective squeaky wheel. This, too, could save you. If something goes against what your understanding of the treatment plan is then do not go along with it until you have clarification. Somebody may have written the wrong name or room number on the test request.[9]

The Power to Lead

An illness can be the time for those affected to reflect on their humanity, faith and beliefs. They may suddenly decide to help others by teaching, or leading support groups. They may explore activities they never had time for. Someone who spent their time working and obtaining great wealth may want to now give money to fund charities they never would before. They change from thinking material things are the most important goal to realizing there is a greater good. They realize what is most important for them to live each day fully.

Education

Many times the need for more knowledge will be an urgent need for the person with a serious or life threatening illness. The two categories of educational pursuit are secular and spiritual. The desire for more secular education can stem from many causes. The desire for a secular education can stem from the need to complete an earlier goal that was deterred by unforeseen circumstances. Someone who has never finished high school and gotten their diploma may suddenly want to complete this goal. Others may want to leave a legacy to their children or grandchildren to emphasize the importance of secular education by completing their college degree.

The urge for spiritual education usually has a different reason behind it. Serious or life threatening illnesses bring our earthly mortality front and center to all we do. Each day is faced with what if this does not work what then. Even those who have mocked the reality of God and his son Jesus will ask questions and seek information about Him. This is a great opportunity for the faith community to step in and gently educate and lead those willing to Christ. We as ministers to this population need to be flexible in our classes and teachings. Time may be limited. Give the information that is crucial and leave the rest for those who are not in critical need of the main focus. Move the class to different days and times, go to the homes and teach, bring just a few folk with you, or do one to one teaching. Include the family and caregivers if desired. Ask what is needed and how they wish to have the information given, i.e. a lecture, a book, on the internet, a video, and the radio. During this time salvation and the strength of God's presence is crucial for the living of the life now as it prepares us for the life to come.

Chapter III

Caregiving During Illnesses

Caregiving is taking care of someone who is sick or unable to take care of themselves. Many persons who are performing the duties of caregiving do not identify themselves as care givers. The book the Unbroken Circle, by James L. Brooks published in 2009 states that at the time it was published there were 44 million caregivers in the United States.[2]

A Prayer for Caregivers: A Catholic Prayer

Bless those who take care of the sick.

In their own time of need, may they receive

A hundredfold of the blessings they have given.

Care is being provided in the caregiver's home as well as the recipients' home. Caregiving is also provided in facilities such as Assisted Living Facilities, Rest Homes, Skilled Nursing and Hospice Facilities. Many families have to provide caregiving via long distance by hiring others to do the local care. No matter what the setting, being a caregiver has challenges and it can have opportunities.

Challenges of the responsibility of caregiving can lead to stress and grief. Let's explore this together. If you have been a care giver or observed others in this role, think about how caregiving affected the caregiver. How did others especially the faith communities help? How ineffective was the faith community during these times? A list of some challenges of caregiving and the stress it creates follows. When ministering to care givers observe the challenges and stresses they experience and add to this list.

Caregiving

Challenges of:	Creates:
Administering Medications	Stress: Due to self neglect
Wound Care	Fear of doing something wrong/causing harm
Physical labor of moving person	Disgruntled family members
Giving IV, Tube feedings, complicated treatments	Grief
Complete care of the home	Isolation-no one visits
Paying all the bills	Loss of former self
Finding rides because you do not drive	

Physical Stress

The majority of the care given to those with serious and life threatening illnesses are not covered by insurance and agencies. They are performed by spouses and family members usually children and grandchildren. Sometimes after leaving the hospital and skilled nursing facility there may be short term intermittent home care services. But the caregiver must still provide the majority of the 24/7 physical care. We must remember many of the caregivers are not in good physical health themselves. This gives us as the community of faith more reason to minister to this neglected population. Many caregivers will complain that they are going to the hospital and doctors themselves because of physical ailments such as headaches, loss of appetite etc. Many times this is looked on as the caregiver trying to get attention or turn the attention to their self. Now there may be times when this is true. But most times the challenges of taking care of someone have created stress showing itself in these physical symptoms.[3]

Emotional Stress

Caregivers are also subject to psychological and emotional stress. Many report they are afraid of what to say. Afraid they will say the wrong thing. Or they are afraid they will do the wrong thing. They are afraid they will forget an important medication or treatment. They are terrified the rest of the family who is never around will blame them when things go wrong. Care givers can become depressed; have anxiety, and fear. Because they are exhausted they may have bursts of anger, forget to give important treatments, miss their own doctor appointments, forget to take their medications or fail to pay bills. Old habits of alcohol and drug abuse that were conquered decades before may reoccur, as a way to escape the pain caregiving brings.

When someone has to care for a loved one who is ill daily tasks become enormous chores.

This is the opportunity for ministers and the faith community to care for the caregiver. Give care to the caregiver by asking about how they are coping with the care. Ask if there are any helpers coming in. Discuss areas that are lacking and other needs not met for the patient and the care giver. Listen between the words said and discern what the issues are. If not talk with your parishioners about organizing assistance based on the needs you have identified. Many times we give up too soon when the caregiver does not speak right up and tell us what they need.[6]

Let's read a familiar passage from the Bible.

Luke 5:17:20 And it came to pass on a certain day, as he was teaching, that there were Pharisees and doctors of the law sitting by, which were come out of every town of Galilee, and Judaea, and Jerusalem: and the power of the Lord was *present* to heal them. And, behold, men brought in a bed a man which was taken with palsy: and they sought *means* to bring him in, and to lay *him* before him. And when they could not find by what *way* they might bring him in because of the multitude, they went upon the housetop, and let him down through the tiling with *his* couch into the midst before Jesus. And when he saw their faith, he said unto him, Man, thy sins are forgiven thee.

These men were determined to get their friend to the Master. The Bible does not give us the conversation among the man and his friends. I can imagine in my mind that the man told them do not worry about it I will see the Master another day, it is too much trouble for you. I can see them saying, no we will find a way.

How many of us wiggle out of visiting, advocating or ministering to the sick when they say it is okay come another day?

Spiritual Stress and Strain

Many caregivers do not get the opportunity to attend their church because they cannot leave their loved one alone. Sometimes there are medications or treatments that must be given so that they cannot leave home. They may feel isolated from the faith community because of lack of fellowship. When we do visit we need not blindly quote scripture that soon sounds like a commercial on the T.V. drowned out by the "noise" of obligations and duties.

Opportunities of Caregiving

Yes there are many challenges when giving care but there are also some opportunities. Many caregivers will grow in several different ways while they care for a loved one. They will learn many new skills by providing hands on care. They may develop a stronger faith and discover spiritual strengths as they grow deeper in faith. They may find new support in family and other networks. We as

Christians, ministers to those who are ill must assist those who have a more positive experience as well as those who do not. In the United States we assume that everyone has insurance. For those who have insurance we think all the bills are paid so you should have no financial worries.

Most of us do not know that Medicare pays very little, and most retirees do not have a secondary insurance. With the new Medicare plans they pay less than regular Medicare in many instances. The thought is that if you are working or have a private insurance then you really have it made. Rarely do we think about the fact that the caregiver may have to cut their working hours or stop working completely to take care of their loved one. This may then take the household income from two working persons down to no one working. Unless you have been in the hospital in intensive care, on the heart floor or had surgery you may have no idea how expensive it can be. Most hospital admissions on a regular floor can cost up to $1,000 daily. The intensive care units and heart care wards can be ten times the regular floor price. Many of those admitted have to get to the hospital by ambulance and the cost of this fee can be astounding. In the area where I practice home health the EMS services bill can be from $400 to $800 one way. Many insurances including Medicare do not cover this cost and when they do, there is a large co-pay charged. Surgery bills, lab bills, medication bills, the individual doctor bills, special tests and x-ray bills are all separate from the hospital bed costs. Caregivers have a lot to be concerned about. Do not for one minute think the person who is sick is not thinking about how much his illness is costing, and affecting the family.

We need to think outside of the normal box and do more than send a card of good thoughts. There is hardly a faith community that does not do a great job when there is a new baby born, or a short lived need. But how well do we do when the situation is for months and years? I am not assuming we can provide all the needs for all that need it but we can do much more than we currently do to relieve some of this burden. We as the community of faith need to first educate ourselves by learning what do as you are doing you are by reading this. The church or group of those who minister to the sick can have someone come to educate them and the members to assure those who are ill and their care givers are taken care of and that we are aware of their needs. We need to know of the services that could assist that the family may not be aware of. Review the list of caregiver challenges and the problems they create again.

Challenges of Caregiving:

Administering Medications

Wound Care

Physical labor of moving person

Giving IV, Tube feedings, complicated treatments

Complete care of the home

Paying all the bills

Finding rides because you do not drive[3]

As you review these think about how overwhelming they are when you must do them all day. How can ministers to those giving care be helpful and effective in our ministry and at the same time alleviate as many of the challenges, stress and grief that occurs for the patient and the caregiver? Earlier the topic of the activities of daily living was discussed. Now think about some of the smaller jobs that are necessary. Garbage must be removed from the house to either be taken to the dump or put out for the city to collect. Who lives nearby that takes out their own garbage or goes to the dump? Medical appointments must be kept. Who goes to the same hospital for appointments or to the same doctor's office? Groceries must be picked up from the store. Who passes the home on their way home or to the store? This is how we become effective in the care of this group in need. Most often the faith community just thinks of visitation as the way to take care of those who are sick. Do not think this is not a valuable thing to do. It is the foundation of ministering to those who are ill, and those who are caring for them. Do not forget the power of laughter. Do not be afraid of being jolly. "The joy of the lord is our strength". Nehemiah 8:10 Then he said unto them, Go your way, eat the fat, and drink the sweet, and send portions unto them for whom nothing is prepared: for this day *is* holy unto our Lord: neither be ye sorry; for the joy of the LORD is your strength.[1] Proverbs 15:13 A merry heart maketh a cheerful countenance: but by sorrow of the heart the spirit is broken.

"Laughter is good medicine." Proverbs 17:22 A merry heart doeth good *like* a medicine: but a broken spirit drieth the bones. Just be mindful of when and where to be jolly, and with whom and about what. There are appropriate and inappropriate times for humor. Many times it is just the medicine that is needed. The great news is that laughter is easily given. Giving a large amount of laughter cannot not cause overdose.

Let's look at several situations that can present special preparation.

Care givers of those who have memory deficits can be especially challenging. When visiting with this person you must remember not to bring attention to the memory loss. Enter by saying hello and wait to see if the person recognizes you. Do not ask, do you know who this is? If the family member says this just say your name and association. For example, I am going to visit with my mother's sister. My mother has been gone from this life over thirty years. I walk in and say. "Hello auntie, this is

Zelda, your sister Louise's oldest daughter." She replies, Louise, how is she? Why didn't she come with you?" I respond with, "She couldn't come today. What a beautiful robe, I remember you like to sew."

Why didn't I just say my mother is dead? I could have followed with, she's been dead for 30 years, and you know that. Here is why this is not a caring response. Obviously my aunt in this example did not remember that my mother was dead. So saying to my aunt her favorite sister was dead would be like she just died. This would be would be a cruel thing to do and as ministers we should be doing all things with the love of Jesus. My aunt would start grieving all over again. By replying as above I did not tell an untruth. I just redirected her thoughts to something pleasant for her. If she had kept asking about my mother I would continue diverting after giving a vague but truthful answer. It is not necessary for a person who has dementia or memory problems to remember exactly everything correctly. If she had remembered that my mother had died, and commented on this I would have replied, yes years ago, remember how you two talked about how I cried all the time as a baby and toddler. Thus you are still diverting to a pleasant subject for her. You get the picture.

It is very exhausting for caregivers when their loved ones have severe memory loss.

There are many different diseases that cause memory loss. You may hear the words Dementia, Alzheimer's, Organic Brain Syndrome, Chronic Brain Syndrome, or Hardening of the Arteries going to the brain. Dementia does not mean the person is mentally ill. It is used by medical professions to describe a group of symptoms the person has not a specific disease.[24] These symptoms can be confusion, memory loss of past and recent events, disorientation, intellectual impairments or similar symptoms.[3] Very low vitamin b12 levels in older adults can cause confusion and forgetfulness and many times this is reversible with medication. In the elderly being confused or disoriented can be the first symptom exhibited when there is an acute infection such as a urine infection or pneumonia. Some diseases that cause dementia are able to be treated and then the dementia goes away. There are two major diseases that cause dementia that are not reversible. The most common is Alzheimer's disease. This disease not only affects the mind but it progresses to the point of total disability. Although many medications have arisen to treat this disease there is no cure at this time and no rhyme or reason as to how each person reacts to this disease and the medications. Vascular Dementia is the second most common disease that causes dementia. This disease is usually the result of multiple strokes within the brain. You may have heard this condition referred to as the hardening of the arteries. Research has now identified that this condition is not the result of the lack of circulation but of strokes. Sometimes early treatment can stop the progression of this type of dementia. Illnesses that cause dementia attack all racial groups, the poor as well as the rich, the meek and the famous. Some persons experience a complete change in personality. My uncle had been a bishop in eastern North Carolina for over 45 years. He could recite the Bible used in his Free Will Baptist Church by memory. I remember while teaching Sunday school or preaching he would say turn to page x and we will read John 1: 12-25 together. He never opened the Bible he just started reciting the word. One day I came from my home to hear him preach and he was in the middle of the sermon and mixed up the scripture. I knew something was wrong. I then approached his wife, my aunt, and she finally unburdened her heart with the things she had been noticing. He was soon diagnosed with vascular and Alzheimer's dementia.

Signs of concern can be, when a loved one goes from being sweet and kind and loveable to being sharp, angry all the time and mean. The person goes from being energetic to lethargic. Once previously calm they have now become demanding, fearful or accusing. Activities that were simple for them to do now become a battle. They may not want to get dressed because it is too difficult to figure out what to do next.

The person may ask the same question repeatedly or ask for someone who is deceased and each time the caregiver must calmly answer. One of our greatest gifts as ministers in these situations can be to give relief to the caregivers and have another church member or person of the faith take them away from the home even if it is just to go across the street. If sitting with the person with memory loss is not a comfortable or a possible thing for you to do consider making a donation to the family to hire someone for a few hours.

Let's explore another situation that creates stress that we can assist with. You are going to visit someone in a facility, a hospital, a nursing home or hospice, they are not related by birth but it is someone you know, this person has cancer and is sitting in a wheel chair. His roommate has a large number of family members in the room with lots of unruly children running around. He is obviously uncomfortable but not saying anything. Look at this possible example of how to handle this common situation.

"Deacon Croom it seems your roommate has a lot of company, would you like to go to a quieter place and talk. I sure would. If you do not mind I will ask the nurse where there is a quiet place to go to talk." Visitor goes to the desk to find a nurse. The buzzer in the room is not activated because the nurse probably could not hear over the noise in the room and the visitor does not want to appear to be telling on the other family even though they obviously have not cared about Deacon Croom. The nurse is found and explanation is given that they need a place to talk quietly, and privately. The nurse assists Deacon Croom to the parlor waiting area and closes the door for privacy. Now Deacon Croom has a visit filled with prayer and conversation.

When you are making a visit listen with an open heart. You know your strengthens. If something is asked or requested that you are not comfortable answering it is okay to say, I am not sure or I don't know but let me write this down or let me call Rev. Clifton etc. None of us are expected to know all the answers. Use the answer I learned at Bethel Bible College and Seminary, "Let me research that and get back to you on that."

Here are some general guidelines when conducting spiritual support during visitation.

- Be mindful of the setting: look for a quiet area that is private and will be comfortable in expressing spiritual feelings and needs.

- Ask permission to discuss spirituality, the Bible, faith, or hope etc. Phrase the words to match the situation for the person you are visiting. Saved or not saved, religious or not religious.

- Be there, be present. Don't let fear of not knowing what to say overcome you. Always pray before entering to ask for God's guidance.

- Ask open supportive questions so the person leads the direction and knows you care by your attention.

- Be acceptable and prepared for the range of emotions that may surface. You may witness, joy, sadness, lack of concern, to worry, happiness or anger.

- Use spiritual references in a calm non-judgmental manner.

- Be patient. Do not expect instant changes or acknowledgement of the information you have given. Each person's timetable and acceptance time is different. [3]

Avoid Clichés

Listen to the intent behind the words. Many Christians quote the wonderful scriptures given for our use in the time of trouble. But these words said over and over to someone in need for more week after week and year after year can sound like a Sunday school recital. Assist the person, if able or do it for them, to rewrite the scriptures that relate to them or their situation so they become a personalized comfort to them straight from God.[28] Here are some examples my sister Annette and I have used during difficult times in our lives.

Psalms 62

¹Truly my soul waiteth upon God: from him *cometh* my salvation. ²He only *is* my rock and my salvation; *he is* my defense; I shall not be greatly moved. ³How long will ye imagine mischief against a man? ye shall be slain all of you: as a bowing wall *shall ye be, and as* a tottering fence. ⁴They only consult to cast *him* down from his excellency: they delight in lies: they bless with their mouth, but they curse inwardly. Selah. ⁵My soul, wait thou only upon God; for my expectation *is* from him. ⁶He only *is* my rock and my salvation: *he is* my defense; I shall not be moved. ⁷In God *is* my salvation and my glory: the rock of my strength, *and* my refuge, *is* in God. ⁸Trust in him at all times; *ye* people, pour out your heart before him: God *is* a refuge for us. Selah. ⁹Surely men of low degree *are* vanity, *and* men of high degree *are* a lie: to be laid in the balance, they *are* altogether *lighter* than vanity. ¹⁰Trust not in oppression, and become not vain in robbery: if riches increase, set not

your heart *upon them.* [11]God hath spoken once; twice have I heard this; that power *belongeth* unto God. [12]Also unto thee, O Lord, *belongeth* mercy: for thou renderest to every man according to his work.

My personal version:

Lord when difficult times and seasons come I can patiently wait for your resolution. Only you have the answers for my life and I wait upon you because I trust you. Lord please hold me steady and tightly while I wait for my difficult time and season to end. I am confident that you will fight all battles for me. Your word says the Lord also will be a refuge for the oppressed, a refuge in the time of trouble. Have mercy on me Lord. Consider my trouble which I suffer from them that hate me. I will praise thee my Lord, with my whole heart. I will not depend on man for this is only resolved through you. I trust in you for my protection. You are my rock. You know the beginning and the end of all my situations. Forgive me for the sin I commit daily and wash me clean again by the blood of you r son Jesus, Lord. I praise your work in my life through Jesus. Lord, I thank you for giving me understanding that I do not need to fix this situation myself. You are here to fix it all. You know the outcome and will protect me and lead me in the right direction as I cannot see the way to go. I will sing songs of joy to you Lord, preserve me o, God for in thee do I put my trust, Psalms16:1 I will bless you Lord for you have given me counsel. I will not interfere in the solving of this situation in my life. I will praise you as you take care of them for me. I have learned my lesson form rushing in and trying Lord, to solve things myself. All I did was hurt myself. I know now you will protect me and I trust in you. You Lord are my defense from the destruction of the enemy. You are my shield from his fiery darts. You are my fortress from his army of demons. I will not be moved from trusting you. Lord thank you for giving me salvation through Jesus Christ. My belief that you are my refuge during these troublesome times is what keeps me going.

Now read the scripture that most Sunday schools teach its young.

Psalms 23:1-6

¹The LORD *is* my shepherd; I shall not want. ²He maketh me to lie down in green pastures: he leadeth me beside the still waters. ³He restoreth my soul: he leadeth me in the paths of righteousness for his name's sake. ⁴Yea, though I walk through the valley of the shadow of death, I will fear no evil: for thou *art* with me; thy rod and thy staff they comfort me. ⁵Thou preparest a table before me in the presence of mine enemies: thou anointest my head with oil; my cup runneth over. ⁶Surely goodness and mercy shall

follow me all the days of my life: and I will dwell in the house of the LORD forever.

Now read my personalized version.

Father God, thank you for providing shelter, food, pretty things, a job, friends, family and other wants. I realize you did not do this because I deserve them, you did it because you love and care for me. You desire to give me all my heart wants and I thank you in advance for this. Lord thank you for giving me a restful place to sleep and live without worry as I sleep peacefully each night. I know it all comes from you Lord. Thank you for a renewal in you through the restful peace you have given me. I can refresh and recharge my soul to walk in righteousness for you. Lord thank you for a mind to do the right things and follow you. Thank you for the sill to follow your word and grow in grace as I learn more about you and your word. I cannot thank you enough for carrying me when trouble is all around me, sickness, sorrow, and all the difficult time of my life. Thank you for letting me know I can glorify you during these valley times. Because of my faith in you I am not afraid during these times because I know you are there. I feel your arms of comfort around me. Even through my tears and despair I can come out of this pain by knowing you are there to comfort me and wipe my tears one at a time as they fall. I praise you for the Holy Spirit and your Son Jesus' sacrifice for me so that I would not be alone in the valley of the shadow of death time s of my life. Lord for blessing me during the times when my enemies are attacking me I thank you. You show them I am protected by supernatural holy hands and they cannot touch what is yours. You bless me while they are attacking until my cup is running over the top because it is over filled. You baffle the enemy by this and I praise you. Lord as long as I keep your word and do as you have requested I know you will be with me, your grace and your mercy and the goodness will be with me daily. I will stay steadfast on you. Thank you, Lord for being with me always, and forever. I praise and adore you. Here is another example of how to take the scriptures of Psalms and make it personal.

Psalm 62

[1]Truly my soul waiteth upon God: from him *cometh* my salvation. [2]He only *is* my rock and my salvation; *he is* my defence; I shall not be greatly moved. [3]How long will ye imagine mischief against a man? ye shall be slain all of you: as a bowing wall *shall ye be, and as* a tottering fence. [4]They only consult to cast *him* down from his excellency: they delight in lies: they bless with their mouth, but they curse inwardly. Selah. [5]My soul, wait thou only upon God; for my expectation *is* from him. [6]He only *is* my rock and my salvation: *he is* my defence; I shall not be moved. [7]In God *is* my salvation and my glory: the rock of my strength,

and my refuge, *is* in God. [8]Trust in him at all times; *ye* people, pour out your heart before him: God *is* a refuge for us. Selah. [9]Surely men of low degree *are* vanity, *and* men of high degree *are* a lie: to be laid in the balance, they *are* altogether *lighter* than vanity. [10]Trust not in oppression, and become not vain in robbery: if riches increase, set not your heart *upon them.* [11]God hath spoken once; twice have I heard this; that power *belongeth* unto God. [12]Also unto thee, O Lord, *belongeth* mercy: for thou renderest to every man according to his work.

This is my sister's, Annette Williams, personal version of this Psalm.

Lord God, no matter how long it takes I wait on you. I arrest my mind, my will and my emotions and put them in check to wait on you. Only you can save me, only You have the answers for my life and the lives of those you have placed on my heart. Yes Lord I wait on you alone.

Nothing will take me away for you my God; you are the stability in my life. You are the standard by which all things are measured for me, You are my rock! Yes, Lord anyone who brings harm against me will be slain. They may stand for but a moment, but soon will fall just like an unstable fence without a proper foundation. Those who seek to destroy me only speak to me to see me fall, they love to lie and flatter me but in their heart they curse me. I must pause and think carefully about the intents of man, as your word says I can only trust in you, so therefore in you is where I place my trust. I speak to my soul and I command it to wait only on God, I can only expect Him to be true to His word and to protect me and help me and provide for me. Once again I say you are my rock Lord, only you defend me. Nothing shall move me away from your shelter and protection. Whenever I have situations arise I know that you God, you are my refuge. I can run to you and be saved. You are solid and strong. I place myself fully in your arms of protection. No matter what happens, no matter what I see or hear I put my whole trust in you. I give you all my concerns, all my fears, all my hopes, all my dreams. You are my refuge and I pause to marvel at the wonder of who you are. Dear Lord let me not put stake in any man's position whether high or low because when they are both measured they are both of little importance. And even so let me not put myself ant higher or lower than I should because position does not matter to you in the way it does to man. Help me stay balanced in all my thinking and in all I do. Lord help me not to trust in taking from others with evil intent and help me not to trust in wealth , riches are not stable like you are Lord, for in a moment they too, can vanish away. I only want to put my trust in you because you are the only truth and constant in my life. Your voice has spoken to me the power is Yours. I believe your word and proclaim that power belongs to you. And also you control mercy, it is Yours. You give mercy as you see fit. I trust that you are just and I thank you for the mercy that you have given to me. I approach your trine boldly to obtain mercy for those in my breastplate prayers and ask you to be merciful to them and help them gently be your spirit to come to the full knowledge of your truth and the life you have for them in Christ Jesus. Amen[29]

I challenge you to take some of the scriptures that comfort you and personalize them. I have many I have done and they have made me know and feel God was beside me in the times or seasons of growth and trials.

There are many other comforting passages that you can use to assist those in need by making them personal for the individual. This will also give you a purpose for the visit. Not a just a reason to say you went to visit. You will be there for a purpose. You will really be there. Assisting others in connecting with God during difficult times when they may not be able to because of illness is a ministry we all need to do to educate ourselves in and practice. [9]

Another ministry that tends to be overlooked by our faith community is relief of the caregiver in the hospital, rest home, skilled nursing facility or hospice. When you go to offer respite time to the caregiver have an activity to do so the person you are sitting with does not feel like they have to entertain you. Bring a Bible or book to read. Complete some sewing or needlework project. Work on your sermon or just pray silently. This lets the sick person know it is okay to nap. If they want to talk let them discuss whatever they wish.

Counseling Opportunities:

The Oxford English Dictionary defines counseling as to give advice, especially that given formally: give professional help and advice to (someone) to resolve personal or psychological problems. Christian counseling is pastoral counseling which draws upon psychology and Christian teaching.[24]

Christian counseling it is to give advice, especially that given formally: give professional help and advice to (someone) to resolve personal, psychological problems, and spiritual problems.

A pioneer of Christian Counseling is Jay E. Adams. He published his book "Competent to Counsel" in 1970. He named his type of counseling nouthetic counseling a form of pastoral counseling. This type of counseling is based on the belief that all counseling should be based solely upon the Bible. But Adams went on to say that it is also based on the sin of the person. Thus the techniques he created did not create a soothing and helpful solution as the Bible teaches. The clergy found fault with this thinking, as I do. Counseling or advice given to a person should give comfort to the recipient. The recipient of counseling should feel they have been given direction or shown how to find the answers for their situation. Even if the answers are that there is no solution. Even non-Christian psychologists agree that Jay E. Adams' nouthetic counseling can do considerable harm to those seeking counsel. [31]

So how are we to give counsel? First you have to go to the person. Most of those confined to home, a hospital or nursing home do not have an abundance of visitors during the week days. When asked what the most troubling thing there is about being confined many will state the loneliness and lack of visits from friends, family and the church. The caregiver or family member may ask to come to you just to get away from the issues at home. This is fine because then there are no interruptions that they must deal with. Remember when asked to give counsel the first thing is to listen with a prayerful heart. You may see emotions that have never been exhibited by the person in your presence. No signs of shock or disapproval should be expressed.

During times of distress and difficulty raw emotions will be expressed in a multiple of ways. You may hear language that is not pleasant or descriptions that you may not be comfortable with. This is not the time for correction. It is the time for listening and letting them get it off their chest so to speak. Then when the raw emotion has subsided acknowledge the "rawness". You can gently say things like, "Sister Janie I know this must be a very difficult problem for you to use that language from before you got saved." Or "Brother James I have seen the love you have exhibited toward your wife over the years this must be very hurtful to you when she does not remember who you are." Remember each person is an individual and each feeling is real for that individual.

Most times when ministering to caregivers or the patient you will find all that is needed is a listening heart, to hear what is needed to be said without judgment or reply. Grab a hand, touch a shoulder, give a hug, stroke a forehead, and nod in understanding. Don't be ready to leave because a tear may come or anger flows out, it is okay to cry along if you are tender hearted, I am.

I stopped doing home care for a few years because I cried all the time and I felt it was not good for the patients or families. I missed this work and went back, my first patient passed away and I told the caregiver, her daughter, how saddened I was for her loss. As tears flowed down my cheeks, I wiped them telling her I was sorry for crying. She looked me straight in the face and said it is okay that you are crying this is just an example of the loving care you gave my Mom flowing from your heart. It means you cared.[21] This is what caregivers and those in need should feel from us at every visit we make. They should feel we cared for them and about them, their problems and their difficulties.

What if visiting someone with dementia or a caregiver who is not handling things as well is just too much for you to feel confident in your ministering to them? What if you are afraid of the hospital and the tubes and equipment that is all around the patient? Know that it this is okay to feel this way. Everyone is not a nurse or ready to embrace medical things. Find your comfort area to minister and offer assistance. For the times you are not comfortable, have a buddy to go with you to visit those that you feel are more than you can do alone. You can pray or read comforting scripture so you do not have to focus on the medical stuff. Simply laying on hands, listening to them, or just sitting quietly means the most when you are ill. I remember just recently I was rushed to the hospital via ambulance for chest pain. I was sent to the cardiology floor after being in the emergency room for hours in off and on pain. My adopted mother Josie and father Reggie and the minister from my church came to sit with me until my sister Valerie could come. The most pleasant things I remember about this challenging episode of my life were: 1. Opening my eyes and seeing they were there praying for me even as I slept, 2. Waking up and seeing Valerie in the chair beside my bed hovering over me watching my every breath. I remember thinking it is so good to be loved. Remember, it is just being there that makes the difference. It makes the difference in the person feeling cared about and feeling left all alone. I know you say they are not alone, they have the Lord. I know I had the Lord when I was in UNC hospitals not knowing for sure what was wrong with my heart and knowing I had too much work left to do. But I was glad that the Lord sent some humans as His appointed angel to be with me. This is how the being there on the side in the correct way feels to the person in the bed. The Bible gives us many examples of how to counsel those in need.

Other Tips for Offering Spiritual Support While Visiting the Ill

❖ Do not wear perfumes or colognes, or scented lotions. They can make many persons ill. This will stop all conversation because they need you to leave before they get sicker.

❖ Be Present: you do not have to have any answers, just listen and write down questions you cannot answer to get back to them. You are there that is the important part.

❖ Give the person who is ill the chance to express what is on their heart and mind to a willing listening ear. Also give them a chance to discuss concerns, and questions.

❖ Have no agenda except to offer hope, and compassion.

❖ Identify yourself clearly in a soft yet audible voice.

- ❖ Sit near the person but never on the bed. Do not stand and hover over the person.

- ❖ Pray for the patient, family, and those who are providing care.

- ❖ Avoid Clichés: "It is God's will" or "Everything happens for a reason" tend to shut down conversation. Instead listen for the thoughts and feelings behind the statements made.

- ❖ Offer compassionate support: Keep your focus on the other person: his stories, questions, thoughts and feelings; be engaged in all that is said through your expression of support, encouragement or love.

- ❖ Use spiritual references as appropriate: Use your knowledge and experiences with the person to offer prayers, readings or songs. Ask them their favorite.

- ❖ Remember that you are not in this alone: Know you comfort zone and limits. Ask for your pastor and his ministerial staff when needed.

❖ Reminder that bears repeating: Respect the fact that each person deals with spiritual issues in individual time and ways. Your time table may not be their time table, be patient[3]

When visiting those with serious illness and/or life threatening illness conversation is very important. The time spent while visiting is valuable to the one receiving the visit as well as the one giving the time. It must include attention, sincerity, patience, active listening, and effective communication skills. The tone of voice and inflection of the words can change the meaning of what you are trying to convey. In order to be effective in achieving productive conversation the use of open ended questions is helpful. Open ended questions are those which require more than a yes or no answer. Think of phrasing questions using the words, how, and what instead of do, did or were. You sense the person is upset, but you want to make sure this is true.

Ask how do you feel right now? Instead of are you feeling upset about something? To find out what activities you could do with him ask what activities do you enjoy doing? Instead of do you like to read the Bible?

Questions that are open ended make good conversation starters for when you visit someone you do not know well. For example; what was it like living on a farm when you were a child? Then you can use phrases to expand the conversation. In others words keep him talking. Tell me more about how you sheared the sheep. Ask questions when things are not clear. I know you just told me but could you go over again why the nurse upset you. When the person directs the conversation to you or your life you can redirect by using things like, thank you for your concern but I would really like to hear about how your daughter is doing with her twins. Or try, you mentioned that you had a pet hog on the farm.

When the conversation gets into difficult areas where the person may be asking for your advice or opinion steer away from answering by review of past or present efforts of problem solving they have used. What did you do when this occurred last year? Have you talked to anyone about this? What have you done so far? What choices do you feel you have?

When visiting the sick, never seem rushed but never over stay. What are the signs you can see that it may be time to leave? The family is nodding or the patient is asleep. The nurses are in and out frequently doing treatments. The meal tray has come in. Exit by saying a brief prayer and that you will visit again and tell them the day. Remember to keep the appointment or call to reschedule if something major comes up.

The Practice of Anointing and the Laying on of Hands as a Part of Visitation

In our Christian walk, we have several doctrines and ordinances that we believe and practice; and there are blessings in the Bible that we hold to be true because the Bible says so and the Bible we believe is the inerrant word of GOD. Two of the doctrines that we practice as believers are anointing and the laying on of hands. The anointing of the sick is practiced by many Christian based faiths communities. The laying of the hands where the person praying touches the one being prayed for is often associated with anointing. Or this practice may be a part of prayer. [31]Before anointing or laying hands on someone always ask for permission from the person who is receiving the prayer and/or their caregiver just as you would ask if they would like prayer. Even if you know the person it may not be the time or they may be in pain or discomfort and not able to tolerate touch or anointing. Also remember to only use unscented anointing oil. Fragrances can make many people very ill. Even those who have never had an issue before may have a violent reaction to fragrances. Some teach that the anointing can only be done by the Clergy while others make it a part of all whose ministry is caring for those who have spiritual needs for prayer. So before asking would the person like to be anointed find out their beliefs. Some faiths believe that physical healing is a result of the practice of anointing. Prior to anointing someone that is not of your faith find out if this is their belief. You do not want to be blamed for the outcomes of your anointing. There are other faiths that believe anointing is a spiritual event and may not result in healing if this is not in God's plan. The doctrine from God's word follows:

James 5: 14-16 Is any sick among you? let him call for the elders of the church; and let them pray over him, anointing him with oil in the name of the Lord: And the prayer of faith shall save the sick, and the Lord shall raise him up; and if he have committed sins, they shall be forgiven him. Confess *your* faults one to another, and pray one for another, that ye may be healed. The effectual fervent prayer of a righteous man availeth much.

God uses doctors, and medicines for the healing of our bodies; and divine healing may be received thru the laying on of hands by elders, or believers, as we discussed earlier, or healing may be received by the prayer of faith. Divine healing has been provided for us in the crucifixion of our Lord Jesus Christ.

The thought of touching someone who is sick is another area that can bring discomfort to many of the faith community. The human touch is so very important for those who already feel disconnected from the rest of the world. It is even worse when their spiritual advisors appear to be afraid to touch them. When visiting in the hospital or a skilled nursing facility the nursing staff can be your guide as to whether protective gowns, masks or gloves are needed when you are visiting. If no special care is required do not be concerned. In the event you touch the patient or things in the room, just be sure to wash your hands or use hand sanitizer before and after touching the person or areas in the room. The concern is not that you may get sick but it is just a good hygienic practice.

During the beginning of the aids epidemic patients diagnosed with this disease talked about how they felt they were lepers. The ones who were supposed to love them are the ones who were afraid to visit or touch them. Many times they died alone and or with only the nursing staff in mask, gowns, glove, etc. How many souls did not get the chance of salvation because of unwarranted fear? We now have the technology and the medical research that gives us the correct information to understand how the disease spreads.

Jesus was friend to all with diseases that the world was afraid of. *Matthew 10:6-8* But go rather to the lost sheep of the house of Israel. And as ye go, preach, saying, The kingdom of heaven is at hand. Heal the sick, cleanse the lepers, raise the dead, cast out devils: freely ye have received, freely give.

Luke 7:11-15 And it came to pass, as he went to Jerusalem, that he passed through the midst of Samaria and Galilee. And as he entered into a certain village, there met him ten men that were lepers, which stood afar off: And they lifted up *their* voices, and said, Jesus, Master, have mercy on us. And when he saw *them,* he said unto them, Go show yourselves unto the priests. And it came to pass, that, as they went, they were cleansed. And one of them, when he saw that he was healed, turned back, and with a loud voice glorified God.

The laying on of hands is an elementary doctrine.[31] The Laying on of hands can be by a church elder, or a born again believer.

Hebrews 6:1-3 Therefore leaving the principles of the doctrine of Christ, let us go on unto perfection; not laying again the foundation of repentance from dead works, and of faith toward God, Of the doctrine of baptisms, and of laying on of hands, and of resurrection of the dead, and of eternal judgment. And this will we do, if God permit.[1]

The laying on of hands is used several ways; impartation of the gift of the Holy Spirit, to receive the Holy Ghost and separation for Ministry.[30]

1 Timothy 4:14 Neglect not the gift that is in thee, which was given thee by prophecy, with the laying on of the hands of the presbytery.

Acts 8:15-17 Who, when they were come down, prayed for them, that they might receive the Holy Ghost: (For as yet he was fallen upon none of them: only they were baptized in the name of the Lord Jesus.) Then laid they *their* hands on them, and they received the Holy Ghost.

Acts 6:2-6 Then the twelve called the multitude of the disciples *unto them*, and said, It is not reason that we should leave the word of God, and serve tables. Wherefore, brethren, look ye out among you seven men of honest report, full of the Holy Ghost and wisdom, whom we may appoint over this business. But we will give ourselves continually to prayer, and to the ministry of the word. And the saying pleased the whole multitude: and they chose

Stephen, a man full of faith and of the Holy Ghost, and Philip, and Prochorus, and Nicanor, and Timon, and Parmenas, and Nicolas a proselyte of Antioch: Whom they set before the apostles: and when they had prayed, they laid *their* hands on them.

The Laying on of hands was and is also used in the area of healing. It is usually associated with prayer. Jesus himself practiced this doctrine.[30]

Mark 5:35-41 While he yet spake, there came from the ruler of the synagogue's *house certain* which said, Thy daughter is dead: why troublest thou the Master any further? As soon as Jesus heard the word that was spoken, he saith unto the ruler of the synagogue, Be not afraid, only believe. And he suffered no man to follow him, save Peter, and James, and John the brother of James. And he cometh to the house of the ruler of the synagogue, and seeth the tumult, and them that wept and wailed greatly. And when he was come in, he saith unto them, Why make ye this ado, and weep? the damsel is not dead, but sleepeth. And they laughed him to scorn. But when he had put them all out, he taketh the father and the mother of the damsel, and them that were with him, and entereth in where the damsel was lying. And he took the damsel by the hand, and said unto her, Talitha cumi; which is, being interpreted, Damsel, I say unto thee, arise.

The apostles practiced this as documented in the following scriptures.[30]

Acts 28:8-9 And it came to pass, that the father of Publius lay sick of a fever and of a bloody flux: to whom Paul entered in, and prayed, and laid his hands on him, and healed him. So when this was done, others also, which had diseases in the island, came, and were healed:

Acts 19:11-12 And God wrought special miracles by the hands of Paul: So that from his body were brought unto the sick handkerchiefs or aprons, and the diseases departed from them, and the evil spirits went out of them.

The Jewish Prayer for the sick is an example of a prayer ritual that is similar to those that are practiced by many faiths when visiting the sick.

Mi Sheberakh: May the One Who Blessed
May the One who blessed our ancestors---
Patriarchs Abraham, Isaac, and Jacob,
Matriarchs Sarah, Rebecca Rachel, and Leah---
bless and heal the one who is ill:
_____(name of patient)_____
son/daughter of _____
May the Holy Blessed One
overflow with compassion upon him/her,
to restore him/her,
to heal him/her,
to strengthen him/her,
to enliven him/her.
The One will send him/her, speedily,
a complete healing---
healing of the soul and healing of the body—
along with all the ill,
among the people of Israel and all humankind,
soon,
speedily, without delay,
and let us all say: Amen![2]

There are some ministries that have a small token they give as a reference point for prayer.

The United Church of Chapel Hill has a Prayer Shawl Ministry. They make handmade prayer shawls also called comfort or peace shawls to give to those who are sick and shut in to show their love and support. Others make quilts, blankets and throws for warmth and comfort. When the completed item is delivered it is accompanied by a letter or prayer. The following is the prayer for healing sent to members of the United Church of Chapel Hill, NC:

Prayer for Healing
In the beginning , creating God,
you formed my being.
You knit me together
in my mother's womb.
To my flesh and blood
you gave the breath of life.
O loving One,
renew me this day in your love.
Grant me life
as a gift if your faithfulness.
Grant me light to journey by.

149

Grant me hope to sustain me.
May this mantle be for me
when I am cold and weary.
May it surround me
with comfort when I am suffering.
O Christ who healed the broken
in body and in spirit,
Be with me
and all that suffer this day.
Be with the doctors, nurses,
technicians, chaplains
And all that care for the sick.
Be with the families
and friends of those
Abiding with and
comforting the sick.
May your gentle, yet strong touch
reach out to heal all the
Broken and hurting people and
places in the world.
Amen[2]

Prayer is important. Ask for discernment when you are praying. Be mindful that the person you are praying for may not be able to tolerate a long, drawn out prayer. Prayers need not be 30 or more minutes long. Just get the point across. Do the long petitioning to the Lord with the prayer team or during your private prayer time. A friend of mine who was called to the ministry said his mentor told him during morning worship to keep prayers and sermons short and to the point. After about ten to fifteen minutes minds have wondered.

Some faith communities have developed what are called Creative Support Ministries. They have music ministries that go visit and provide comforting music. They have visited and found the music the person wants to hear. There are other ministries that find the hobby or recreational activity the person loved but can no longer do alone and make sure this activity can be done. When they have a hobby they can no longer do alone they might bring a small project and help them complete.[2] This small gesture can give a joyful break to those in pain.

When my parents died I was 13 years old. I was the eldest child so I experienced the emotional traumas of an adult going through a death of my last parent. I had to go to court to become an emancipated adult so I could make the decision of whether to follow my parents' wishes and have my Aunt become our guardian. The other choice was to allow my uncle, who my parents did not trust, to contest the will and have the court make the final decision as to the outcome. A month later I became very depressed over the burdens put upon me. My aunt was a woman of God who was full of the many gifts. Using her gift of discernment she knew I needed help beyond what she was doing. She decided I need a break to just be a child. She arranged for me to go to a special summer camp. Prior to my parents deaths my two favorite things to do was needlework and planting flowers. When it was time for me to get on the bus to go to camp my Aunt gave me a hug and a kiss and told me she had a surprise for me in my suitcase. I was so happy when I got to camp and pulled out a very fancy and expensive embroidery kit. The note on it said for me to have it all finished by the time I got back. The embroidery kit had the serenity prayer on it with flowers. The finished project was 20 x 30 inches. My Aunt was led by the Lord in giving me this cure. By the time I finished doing that kit I had memorized the prayer by "praying" it the entire summer as I completed it. From that time until today I use this as reminder when ever things get tight. It is displayed in a place of prominence in my home. Since this time I have added many scriptures to my library of comforting words in the time of trouble but this cure from my aunt was the start of my healing through God.

Ministering to Children

What if the person with the serious life threatening illness is a child? There are different needs when a child is suffering severe illness. The age of the child will determine their coping ability. Children will also take cues from the adults around them on how to react with every part of their illness and treatment. In order to minister effectively to this unique group you will need some information before making visits or offering your services. First talk to the parents or guardian to find out what they have told their child. Remember you are not there to tell them what they should or should not be telling their child. Some parents may be very transparent about telling their child details about the disease they have and the treatment in a manner and language they feel the child can handle. Some may have obviously either not said enough or detailed too much. It is not your place to judge or comment on this to them. If you spiritually feel it is doing harm to the family and child pray about this first and then please find a medical professional that can guide you on the path to take to get the family the assistance they need. Do not be surprised if the child seems to be very technical or have become mini doctors or nurses. This is a very helpful technique used for relieving anxiety with the multiple treatments and procedures that may be occurring. Remember this is not an adult it is still a child. A child is defined as anyone under the age of eighteen years of age although some may still be emotionally a child until twenty four years of age.[24] Children like adults may not understand why they have the illness or the cause of the illness and become very angry or regress to behaviors of an earlier stage in their development.[2] For example a six year old who has been toilet trained for years may start having accidents again. Or a three year old who has not used a bottle at bedtime or had a pacifier for over a year, may scream at the top of their lungs that they want their "Binky" back and refuse to stop the noise until you find the "Binky" just like the one he had. We must support the child, parents and family during these times. Remember the reason for this change is not poor parenting it is the way the child is coping with all the stress of the illness. Our job is to give age-appropriate information to all affected by the child's illness to show we are there and their faith community cares.

Children may not be able to tell you how they are feeling, but they still may have many of the following needs:

- ❖ Accurate, honest information about the illness in clear concise language at a level they can understand

- ❖ What causes the illness if known; if not say so, and can they "give" it to others or did someone give it to them

- ❖ Assurance that what they did, said, did not do was not the cause of the disease or will not make it worse (if this is correct)

- ❖ An understanding of the outcome of the illness

- ❖ Answers to spiritual questions from their clergy, beliefs confirmed by the faith community members

- ❖ Validation of their feelings, thoughts

- ❖ Permission to be a child, and act the part[3]

Chapter IV

The Terminally Ill

The legal and law definition: A terminal illness is generally an active and progressive illness for which there is no cure and the prognosis is fatal. It is defined by the American Cancer Society as an irreversible illness that, without life-sustaining procedures, will result in death in the near future or a state of permanent unconsciousness from which recovery is unlikely.[19] Some examples, among others, of terminal illnesses may include advanced cancer, some types of head injury, and multiple organ failure syndrome. The length of life expectancy may vary from entity to entity.

Wikipedia defines terminal illness as a medical term popularized in the 20th century to describe a disease that cannot be cured or adequately treated and that is reasonably expected to result in the death of the patient within a short period of time.[3] This term is more commonly used for progressive diseases such as cancer or advanced heart disease. In the past few years end stage dementia and Alzheimer's disease as well as neurological diseases such as Lou Gehrig and advanced MS have been added to this list.[19] In popular use, it indicates a disease which will eventually end the life of the sufferer. A patient who has such an illness may be referred to as a terminal patient, terminally ill or simply terminal. Often, a patient is considered to be terminally ill when the life expectancy is estimated to be six months or less, under the assumption that the disease will run its normal course. The six-month standard is arbitrary, best available estimates of longevity may be incorrect. Therefore when the medical doctor has stated that the person is terminal this is not a guarantee that the patient will die within six months. In general, physicians slightly overestimate survival so that, for example, when they inform a person there life expectance is to about six weeks they really feel they would likely die around four weeks.

As a Christian who is a registered nurse working with terminal patients I really have a strong opinion that the medical profession has done a disservice to patients by making predictions on what is God's timeline for each of us. The Cancer Treatment Centers of America have in my opinion handled the question of how much time do I have best by replying, in their commercials they state they do not see an expiration date stamped on your heel. If the truth be told, we all according to the Bible should live as if each day is our last. Even so, many people of great faith have difficulty thinking about the death of themselves or a loved one. It is no wonder then that the providing of effective support for this community is one that is full of struggle for most ministers and the members who assist in the ministry to those at end of life or with terminal illnesses.

Ninety percent of all people die from an illness. Be it unexpected or terminal everyone must cope with the changes that occur before and after the death.[19]

There are many tough questions that will come your way as you attend to the terminally ill. Many will be unspoken but you have to discern when they are to be loud yet silent. I mention a few of them and share others you hear when visiting with your ministry team.

Question to health care providers/ caregivers:

❖ What decisions will I have to make, and what are your recommendations. What assistance will I have to make the right choice?

❖ What will you do about my pain, nausea other symptoms?

❖ Will you tell me the truth about whether the treatment is working or not so I can decide what to do next?

❖ If I stop treatment or am too sick to take anymore will you just drop me and not answer my concerns? [17]

Questions to ministers and those who visit from the faith community:

❖ Do you understand I need to be fed the word and to grow even when I seem very ill physically?

❖ Will you listen and not judge me if I scream, am frustrated and even mad at God?

❖ Will you visit me and support me even when I am vomiting, bald, discolored and unable to respond and never show discomfort?

❖ Will you remember my family and loved ones and help them with their spiritual needs.[17]

Before we continue I want to explore an unspoken topic. What do you do when it is just unpleasant to visit someone because of the home conditions? Well if the concern is the untidiness or in cleanliness of the home never let the person or family know you are in discomfort. When you have prior knowledge of the conditions wear the appropriate clothes. If you did not know them you may have to sit on the cleanest area you can or assure the person you have been sitting a while and would like to stretch out your legs by standing. If odors are what makes it a challenging visit then I hope this story will be of assistance. When I was a nursing home inspector I had to go into many nursing homes that were not kept in the cleanest of conditions. Because we made our inspections without notice the staff many times had not cleaned the residents or disposed of the diapers properly. I never wanted to offend the residents because in my experience they were very upset about not being able to care for themselves. I would go to the health food store and purchase a tincture of peppermint. Before entering any of the nursing homes I would put some of the peppermint on my upper lip so I was breathing in the sweet smell of peppermint and not the smells that awaited me. Some of my co-workers used strong mints such as Altoids and would put these in their mouth for about five minutes before entering and then as they entered the home would put it in their upper lip for it to be close to their nostrils.

When a person is very ill having odors is a worry for them. The lack of fluids, the medications and the deterioration of the body changes the body odor. It may also change the ability to smell so they do not know they have an offensive odor about them or their home. Using my technique makes it easier to get up close and show them the love of Christ through us. You can also try vanilla extract and lemon extract. To find which method works for you experiment at home by using one of the remedies. Then go sniffing around your smelliest garbage can. By doing this trial you will know if the remedy you chose will work for you.

The Needs of the Terminally Ill

Those going through the trial of a terminal illness need to be respected for their choices in medical care or the lack of medical care. We as clergy or ministers to those in with this need cannot let our personal feelings or past experiences become a part of our counseling at any time. If the person or family wishes to discuss medical details the following is helpful in order to determine the manner in which to direct your response.

What is expected from the illness? What has the medical team told them? What understanding does the primary caregiver regarding the illness, treatments and outcomes?

It is important to understand there are persons who have a cure from their illness and some have healings. The following chart illustrates the differences.

Cure versus Healing?

Cure:	Healing:
A physical healing from a disease	Refers to finding wholeness
All signs and symptoms are gone never to return	Some symptoms relieved but the illness is not gone

Many times treatment for a terminal illness does result in physical healing without any residual problems. This can be a result of medication, treatments, surgery or God's divine intervention. Then there are times when medication, treatments or surgery gets rid of the terminal illness but leaves a chronic illness that affects the person for a long time.[2] An example of this occurred with my cousin. She was diagnosis with breast cancer. When it was found it had already spread to her lymph nodes. This is a serious condition. She had God's divine healing, medication, treatments and surgery. She is cured from cancer for seven years but she is left with diabetes, and other chronic conditions that are long standing.

There are times when the goal of treatment is to find a way to give the person time to accomplish unfinished things or to alleviate pain or discomfort. This may be referred to as palliative care or symptom management.[19] This means the medical team because of their knowledge of the illness does not know anything else to do for the person. The illness is beyond the stage the doctors feel is curable. As ministers to this group we must understand the medical so we can attend to the spiritual needs of the person on this journey.

The cure path can lead to a testimony for others on faith or the goodness of the Lord. As the healing path can mend a broken family or lead to a healing of the relationship with God or even better yet bring salvation to the family or the person with this pathway.

One term that is important to understand is prognosis. When possible, the doctor uses statistics based on groups of people whose situations are most similar to that of an individual patient. The doctor bases the prognosis on information researchers have collected over many years about hundreds or even thousands of people with cancer. For example: One out of ten persons had a recurrence after treatment within 10 years. For more detail about prognosis is the Fact Sheet from the National Cancer Institute.

Understanding Prognosis and Cancer Statistics:
Questions and Answers
Key Points

• A prognosis gives an idea of the likely course and outcome of a disease (see Question 1).

• Many factors affect a person's prognosis, including the type, location, and stage of the disease; the presence of a chromosomal abnormality or abnormal blood cell counts (for some cancers); and the person's age, general health, and response to treatment (see Question 2).

• When predicting the prognosis, doctors sometimes use statistics based on groups of people whose situations are most similar to that of an individual patient (see Question 3).

• Survival rate is a type of statistic that indicates the percentage of people with a certain type and stage of cancer who survive for a specific period of time after their diagnosis (see Question 3).

• Doctors cannot be absolutely certain about the outcome for a particular patient. In fact, a person's prognosis may change over time (see Question 4).

• The doctor who is most familiar with a patient's situation is in the best position to discuss prognosis, taking into account the individual characteristics of the patient that can affect the overall situation (see Question 5). [33]

1. What is a prognosis?

People facing cancer are naturally concerned about what the future holds. A prognosis gives an idea of the likely course and outcome of a disease—that is, the chance that a patient will recover or have a recurrence of their illness.[19]

2. What factors affect a patient's prognosis?

Many factors affect a person's prognosis. Some of the most important are the type and location of the cancer, the stage of the disease (the extent to which the cancer has metastasized, or spread), and its grade (how abnormal the cancer cells look and how quickly the cancer is likely to grow and spread). In addition, for hematologic cancers (cancers of the blood or bone marrow) such as leukemias and lymphomas, the presence of chromosomal abnormalities and abnormalities in the patient's complete blood count (CBC) can affect a person's prognosis. Other factors that may also affect the prognosis include the person's age, general health, and response to treatment.[19]

3. How do statistics contribute to predicting a patient's prognosis?

When doctors discuss a person's prognosis, they carefully consider all factors that could affect that person's disease and treatment and then try to predict what might happen.[19]

Now this is the medical professionals' opinion, and practice. We are about what God's says.

As believers in Christ we are to always have hope and portray hope to others. The word hope appears 137 times in the KJV of the Holy Bible. Scriptures follow taken from the story of Job a man who suffered painful acute and chronic illness as well as multiple losses of family, servants and possessions. Also I have included a few scriptures from the Psalms, a book with words of praise and comfort.

Job 11:18 And thou shalt be secure, because there is hope; yea, thou shalt dig *about thee, and* thou shalt take thy rest in safety.

Job 14: 7 For there is hope of a tree, if it be cut down, that it will sprout again, and that the tender branch thereof will not cease.

Psalm 16:9 Therefore my heart is glad, and my glory rejoiceth: my flesh also shall rest in hope.

Psalm 31:24 Be of good courage, and he shall strengthen your heart, all ye that hope in the LORD.

When ministering to those with terminal illness use care not to show any signs or express the lack of hope. I was listening to the People's Pharmacy radio program. The guest speaker was an oncology doctor. He revealed how he had not been a doctor that even believed in the power of prayer or the need for hope. One of the stories that changed his belief was a patient that had terminal cancer. The patient prior to treatment asked the doctor to always be honest about his prognosis. The patient's hobby was fishing. He had spent most of his spare time fishing and going on long fishing trips. He wanted the doctor to not say he only had a week etc. He wanted the doctor to just tell him it was time for him to plan a great fishing trip. The doctor thought this was a kind way to do this so when he felt the patient was at the "one month " mark he called the patient and told him to plan his fishing trip soon. The patient died a few days later. This doctor stated he realized then that hope was taken away from the man and he just gave up.

Psalm 31: 13-15 For I have heard the slander of many: fear *was* on every side: while they took counsel together against me, they devised to take away my life. But I trusted in thee, O LORD: I said, Thou *art* my God. My times *are* in thy hand: deliver me from the hand of mine enemies, and from

them that persecute me.

Psalm 119:81 My soul fainteth for thy salvation: *but* I hope

in thy word.

Psalm 119: 114 Thou *art* my hiding place and my shield: I

hope in thy word.

Chapter V

The End of Life: What to Expect

Ecclesiastes 3:1-8

To every*thing there is* a season, and a time to every
purpose under the heaven:
A time to be born, and a time to die; a time to plant, and a
time to pluck up *that which is* planted;
A time to kill, and a time to heal; a time to break down, and
a time to build up;
A time to weep, and a time to laugh; a time to mourn, and a
time to dance;
A time to cast away stones, and a time to gather stones
together; a time to embrace, and a time to refrain from
embracing;
A time to get, and a time to lose; a time to keep, and a time
to cast away;
A time to rend, and a time to sew; a time to keep silence,
and a time to speak;
A time to love, and a time to hate; a time of war, and a time
of peace.

The area no one wants to face is the end of life. But for those of us in Christ we have already prepared for the end of our physical life by ensuring our endless spiritual life.

> **Death is not extinguishing the light; it is only putting out the lamp because dawn has already come.**
> *Philosopher Tagone*

What is meant by the term the end of life? Is it the end of Physical life? We just had the definition of terminal illness given so what is the difference? Think on this; could the end of physical life start at the beginning of life? From the time we are born we never get the last minute back, it is ended. As we age the previous stage has ended. The body is "going downhill" Have you ever seen an old grandfather clock? The kind that has this big pendulum that swings back and forth. The kind that also has this big key that you have to wind up every day to be sure it does not stop keeping time. I remember the grandfather clock my Aunt had. I loved winding that old clock up and watching the pendulum swing back and forth as it made that tic tock sound. One day I had forgotten to wind the clock. Later in the day I noticed it was ticking slower and slower, tic tock, tic tock then tic... tock...... tic....... tock........ tic......... tock, until it finally became silent and stopped. This is how our physical bodies are programmed by God. We all have been given an appointed time at our birth. On the appointed day and time, our clock will run down. For those satisfied through Jesus Christ the experience is only physical death.

There are many physical signs that are different for each person when it comes to the end of life illness. But I do not want to dwell on these there are enough T.V. shows that show this. I don't want any of you to stay away from those who need you most because of concern or fear about the medical details. The discussion of the person's medical details is not the reason we are visiting. Each person will experience the end of life in a personal way. There is no exact way to map out what happens. However there are general similarities of the dying or end of life journey. Some people will have all the signs listed and some will have none of them. As different as God made each of us we will leave the physical body in the same unique ways. But I will review in general the three areas that affect everyone with a terminal illness in about the same way:

Physical Changes:

Persons at the end stage of physical life will have a decreased appetite and thirst. As the illness runs its course the body has a decreased need for food and drink because the body needs less fuel. We should not force or try to guilt those who are in this stage into eating or drinking more than they desire. Giving more fluid than what is needed can cause swelling and discomfort. When visiting someone and they ask for fluids or food always check with the caregiver or medical personnel and ask if they can have some now.

When the person expresses a desired for a specific item, make an effort to inform the caregivers or medical personnel of the request. Many times even when it is difficult an effort is made to give them what they desire as long as it does not create more harm.

Pain was discussed earlier with the patient's pain bill of rights. When visiting the person in the end stage of their disease be aware of the pain control they have. Is what you see the pain management the patient says they desire? If not, become an advocate and ask the caregiver open end questions to determine if there is a need for intervention. For example if the person in pain says they are always hurting, ask if the pain is at a level that he would want the doctor called for a change in treatment for pain. This question helps you know if the patient is tolerating the pain. The caregiver may need education about how to correctly give the medication. The family may not be able to avoid the medication so they are doing as little as possible. As mentioned earlier talking to the medical team may be difficult and the caregiver has given up trying to locate the doctor to inform that the pain medication is not working.

Many of us as we normally age experience daily pain. We keep going and never think anything of it. This also occurs with those who have been in pain for a long time. They soon feel there is no relief for their pain. Many people with would rather hurt than experience the side effects of the medication the doctor has given them. Encourage them to discuss an alternative treatment with their doctors. This is an opportunity to provide ministry on coping with pain as noted in previous chapters.

2 Corinthians 12: 8-10 For this thing I besought the Lord thrice, that it might depart from me.

And he said unto me, My grace is sufficient for thee: for my strength is made perfect in weakness. Most gladly therefore will I rather glory in my infirmities, that the power of Christ may rest upon me. Therefore I take pleasure in infirmities, in reproaches, in necessities, in persecutions, in distresses for Christ's sake: for when I am weak, then am I strong.

Emotional Changes:

One of the first changes that may be seen is called withdrawal. Some will start giving away possessions to specific loved ones.[20] You may be asked to have wayward family members or estranged friends found so they can see them.[18] Withdrawing from activities and increasing sleep or just lying in bed with eyes closed is also observed.[19] Talking is not as important as touching and companionship. This is the time for spiritual energy not physical energy. This is the time to quietly read the comforting scripture. If you know which ones are their favorites read them over and over. If you did the exercise discussed earlier of making the Psalms personal, recite these. Use a sweet, soft calming voice.

John 6:40-48 And this is the will of him that sent me, that every one which seeth the Son, and believeth on him, may have everlasting life: and I will raise him up at the last day. The Jews then murmured at him, because he said, I am the bread which came down from heaven.

And they said, Is not this Jesus, the son of Joseph, whose father and mother we know? how is it then that he saith, I came down from heaven? Jesus therefore answered and said unto them, Murmur not among yourselves. No man can come to me, except the Father which hath sent me draw him: and I will raise him up at the last day. It is written in the prophets, And they shall be all taught of God. Every man therefore that hath heard, and hath learned of the

Father, cometh unto me. Not that any man hath seen the Father, save he which is of God, he hath seen the Father. Verily, verily, I say unto you, He that believeth on me hath everlasting life. I am that bread of life.

John 14:2-3 Let not your heart be troubled: ye believe in God, believe also in me. In my Father's house are many mansions: if *it were* not *so*, I would have told you. I go to prepare a place for you. And if I go and prepare a place for you, I will come again, and receive you unto myself; that where I am, *there* ye may be also.

Those who are Christians as well as those who are not may have a fear of dying that presents as being afraid to go to sleep. Family members may not want to leave because they don't want their loved one to die alone. Minister with comforting scriptures and words, songs touch, investigate to assure the person has accepted Jesus as savior. If not, start working immediately to bring this soul to Christ. Pray without ceasing for this soul.

Cognitive Changes

The research material and all the books I've studied call this next area Cognitive Changes.

This change is disturbing to caregivers because the person who is ill will seem disoriented. They may wander at night and sleep all day. They may get angry at the slightest thing. You will hear things like I am ready to go home or I've packed my bags etc.[15]

As a believer of the Holy Spirit sent to us as a comforter there are two separate circumstances in this area that I have witnessed for persons with cognitive changes:

The first is observed from the saved person and the second is observed when the person is not saved.

Persons who are saved will talk of those who they cared about who have passed on to the other side, they will tell you things that are of God and heavenly places. They may sing verses of hymns remembering all the words when they may no longer know who they themselves are. They may quote scriptures with you as the Bible is read to them. Prayers and praise will be uttered. They may give you words of wisdom that you can feel is not from them but from the Lord. The peace that surrounds them in the mist of physical pain, turmoil, and the death process is loud and clear.

But for those who refuse to accept salvation it is the opposite situation. I have heard those cursing family members as they try to speak Christ to them. Some will confess unspoken sins. This is time to fervently give them the answer of how to have their sins forgiven. Repeat the steps to salvation. The simple ABC's, Accept Jesus as the

Son of God, Believe He died to be our Savior, Confess you're a sinner and ask Jesus to forgive you and come into your heart. If they are only able to speak short phases then ask the questions to them so all they have to do is say or nod yes.

Spiritual Changes

Spiritual changes can go either way; some may feel like God has left them when they are in discomfort. Some may pick fights with the ones they are the closest too or get angry with them. Then some will ask for forgiveness and speak of love in ways they never have before. The hospice SW calls this a time of separating from this world as they prepare to go to the next.

Fancy terms or not this is a trying time for the family and we need to rally around them in gentle ways. Be there but blend in, step up when asked and back away when not.[15]

You may hear them state they are going home. Or they will state they are packing their bags for the trip. Listen and know they may be trying to tell you the end is near and they are going to the next life.

Many of us have a hard time in ministering to this needed population because of our own personal experiences. Be honest with yourself. If you are asked to go visit someone and it is a situation that brings up memories that you cannot put aside do not go see this person. Let the Pastor or ministry team know that this is not a situation you can handle. Now the rest of us must be understanding and not judge any one for realizing their current limitations. We are not to ask why, just accept that we all have the moral right to not visit those we cannot do the best for.

188

Chapter VI

The End of Life Issues

I am standing upon the seashore. A Ship at my site spreads her white sails to the morning breeze and starts for the blue ocean She is an object of beauty and strength. I stand and watch her until at length she hangs like a speck of white cloud just where the sea and sky come to mingle with each other. Then someone at my side says "There, she is gone!"

"Gone where?"Gone from my sight. That is all. She is just a large mast and hull and spar as she was when she left my side and she is just as able to bear her load of living freight to her destined port. Her diminished size is in me., not in her. And just at the moment when someone at my side says: "there she is gone!" there are other eyes watching her coming, and other voices ready to take up the glad shout: "Here she comes!" And that is dying.

Henry Van Dyke

Needs during end of life.

Questions without answers

Why is this happening to me? Why my child, and not me? Doesn't God love me? Why can't I just die? Why? Why? Why?

None of us know the answers to these questions. Do not try to give an answer. Pray and ask if you can pray for the answers. Saying you do not know is a kind and truthful answer.

Questions no one usually asks

The most important thing we of the faith community can do is to have the conversations that really matter before it is too late.

The end of life physician and expert Dr. Ira Bylock has identified five statements that are important during the end of life:[34]

Please forgive me. The family may need to ask for forgiveness for long forgotten offenses. The ministering comforter may become a sounding board for the forgiveness of sins unknown to anyone. Sometimes the burden will be enormous to the one carrying it and you know this is not anything to be concerned about. Do not belittle the confession; give scripture to assure the person all can be forgiven in Christ. Whenever the apology needs to be given to someone who is not around, do your best to find that person. Write down what is to be said to the person and do not misplace it. Relay the message when the person is found. If the message is not one that will be edifying but disturbing do not tell anyone else what is said. It is not our place to speak words that will harm someone. Especially when these are the last words they will hear from the person. Those who are dying will seek forgiveness from God and themselves. Asking for forgiveness is a way to reconcile broken relationships prior to death.

- **I forgive you.** Once someone has offered an apology it is only fitting to say you accept it. It does not mean you have forgotten what was done but if means you have forgiven them as Jesus has forgiven you. By granting forgiveness can bring about healing in broken relationships.

- **Thank You.** Appreciation for what others have done for you is very important during this time. Acknowledging the contributions they have made on your life. The way they changed your life for the good and how you are grateful to them is important.

- **I love you.** Love is an essential part of human life. Taking the time to state this during the end of life is important for both the person leaving as well as the ones left behind. Description of why you love the person is wonderful.

- **Goodbye when it is closer to the end.** The author of this concept says that goodbye comes from the blessing "god be with you." A reminder to us of God's presence in leave taking. As a believer I do not tell someone I know who is a believer goodbye. I always say something like: see you on the other side, see you when my turn comes, or keep singing till I am there to join in. You get the point. However you portray that it is okay for them to leave you is fine. Find the words that are comfortable for you. Ask God for guidance. Trust me the lord will guide you when you rely on Him.

Other Needs at this time

The biggest need is having a caring person around. When visiting you need to prepare by praying for the patient, family, caregivers and yourself. Your goal is to be compassionate, calm and take deep breathes if you start to feel anxious or unsure.

Plan the visit at the convenience for the person. In a facility be aware of the meal time schedules. You may need to ask about medication, or treatment times. Ask for the times when you will not be interrupting a rest period or a difficult time.

Review the previously mentioned points of how to have a productive visit. No perfumes, cologne. Identify yourself clearly. Speak in the appropriate tone and volume. Sit close to the person as you talk with them. Touch communicates when words may fail.

Before you begin the visit acknowledge any other persons within hearing distance and ask permission to continue. Do not let others manipulate the visit. You want to assess the person's wishes not the wishes or opinions of those who speak the loudest or the most frequently.

Additional skills for this stage of ministry include, asking a question about the end of life planning. After asking each question, silently ask God for the discernment to understand the emotions behind the words or lack of words. Then listen with an open heart and mind.

A silent mouth does not mean there are non- hearing ears. Be aware of the energy levels and limit your visit accordingly. Schedule a time to come back to complete the conversation. Small doses of medication are easier to swallow. The same goes for end of life planning.
Spiritual needs should also be addressed. As previously mentioned, ask questions to glean an understanding of their concerns. Offer prayer for specific needs.

The following is a list of what the hospice web site listed a chart for clergy as to what those at the end of life need most:

- Assurance that they will be cared for and not abandoned
- Assistance with making and completing final plans and documents
- Communication with family, friends, caregivers that is honest, open and focused on them being heard and listening.
- Excellence in the delivery of pain control, physical care, comfort, privacy, intimacy, sleep and rest.
- Information that is given is accurate and reliable.
- Permission to feel whatever they are feeling and not be judged or patronized.

Opportunities:

- To discuss impending death with those they choose.

- Discuss final arrangements funeral or cremation without judgment, conflict or argument.

- Tell their stories to leave with those that will listen.

- Explore their spiritual beliefs.

- Reflect on and grief prior losses and current losses.[19]

Bedside Vigils and Rituals

Worship services are just as important at the end of life as it is during the earlier days. Many times the faith community has not thought of this important need. There are many different rituals in other religions that are worthy of reviewing in order to start formulating the appropriate things that can be done in your Christian faith community. In Jewish tradition the dying person may request to recite a prayer of confession, the Vidui. Muslims that are dying recite two articles of faith.[3] Our wonderful Savior left us with a beautiful guide the Holy Bible to be used for all stages and events in live and death. We need to use it at the bedside for His glory and worship. What do you say? It is a time for mourning and sadness. I can see how you feel this way. I had a wonderful friend. Many of those I knew could not understand how she was so loving and kind to me when she was a terror to many others. When I met her I was a true believer and she was not. She had accepted Jesus as a child but never changed her ways. When she told me she was diagnosed with cancer, the first thing that entered my spirit was that she did not really know the Lord in the pardoning of her sins. I think she sensed my worry but never said a word. I helped her with her surgery. I prayer audibly for her and read the Bible while she slept. When she went home I arranged to be her Home Health nurse. I was there three times daily to care for her and praying as I did her care. I remember after a few weeks she asked me why I always prayed before I did the dressing or drew her blood. I replied, God through His son Jesus, gave me this gift and I never want to take His gifts or His mercy for granted. She would make a grunt but never told me to stop. I guess she knew I would just pray silently. A year later when the cancer came back she came to tell me. She said before I tell you what I came for I have to tell you do not have to worry about me anymore. I went to church yesterday and accepted Jesus as my savior for real this time. Then she told me the cancer was back. She lived about another six months or so. As she was passing over to the other side I did as I promised. I read the scriptures and sang hymns to her as she closed her eyes. Her nurse told me to go rest because she was resting. But I knew she was dying, I told her I would see her on the Heaven side and I loved her as the big sister I always wanted. I then whispered in her ear it is okay to go now I will be fine. Jesus will be with me. The nurse called as I arrived home to tell me she ended this life as I got into the elevator.[21] This is what I mean about a ritual. I did this because this was what I saw my Aunt Hattie do for all those times I took her to visit the dying. I have since prayed and asked guidance for each situation. Sometimes I did not get an answer until what I thought was the last minute but God is always on time. You need not do what I did. Ask others who have rituals how they handle it and do what is comfortable to you.

Chapter VII

Taking Care of Business

There are many things every one of us should think about prior to getting to the end of life. Those of the faith community that will be ministering and counseling to those with illnesses and end of life issues need to be educated on these areas.

Nursing Home or no Nursing Home:

Many of us have said to our family members, I will never put you in a nursing home. Or we have said to our family; do not put me in a nursing home. There are times when the honoring of this request is not a loving decision for either one of you. When the only caregiver is too, ill to take care of their loved one, the only course of action may be to move the person to the proper level of care which may be an Assisted Living Facility or a Skilled Nursing Facility. Even if the caregiver is willing, able and available there are certain medical needs and conditions that cannot be provided in the home. When this is the situation, the only course of action will be to move the person to the proper level of care which may be a Skilled Nursing Facility or a Long term Acute Care Facility. Another situation that may result in a discussion about nursing homes is the person who lived alone. There is no one who can live with them to provide the care needed, and the only course of action may be to move the person to the proper level of care which may be a Skilled Nursing Facility or an Assisted Living Facility.[18]

So how do you assist the family? You can only give them the facts to use in making their decision.

Prior to any discussion about a change in residence, assist the family or person who is ill in accepting their limitations. Understanding the limitations of care and ability to do activities of daily living will assist in the explanation of why it is no longer safe for them to be at home at this time. Why should you emphasize, at this time? You have to because we always have faith and hope.

Hebrews 11:1 Now faith is the substance of things hoped for, the evidence of things not seen.

Remember always give hope, even when you do not feel they will ever be home again you do not know this as true only God knows. Have faith, and give hope. Assure them that they have no reason to feel guilty about not being able to do the care needed. The faith community will be asked to provide the 24/7 hour care gaps. Seek the council of the pastor before accepting to become the caregiver that covers the times when the family cannot or will not. Do not commit to what may become a never ending assignment when you know you will not have the persons committed to do the assignments for a long, possibly never ending, time.

There will be times when you will hear complaints about other family members that do not take part in helping. Be very careful not to agree with one opinion or the other. When there are other family members that for whatever reason do not assist in keeping the person in the home make no judgments about this. Just state the facts. They are not helping so this is the reality. Just like the family that belongs to God, believers in Christ, there are members of every family that do not pitch in when they are needed. All we can do is remind them of what Jesus said to his disciples: *Matthews 9: 37-38* Then saith he unto his disciples, The harvest truly *is* plenteous, but the labourers *are* few; Pray ye therefore the Lord of the harvest, that he will send forth labourers

into his harvest.

There are many different levels of care homes for those who are not able to be in their homes during a serious illness. The two main types are Skilled Nursing Facilities or Nursing Homes. These facilities are for people who need chronic or rehabilitative care or long term care. They are no longer classified as acutely ill in need of care that only a hospital can provide. A "nursing home" still provides nursing care by a licensed nurse but not care that must be done in a hospital. Nursing care is their primary need, but they will require continuing medical supervision.

"Adult Care Homes" are facilities that provide care and assistance to people that are no longer able to perform their activities of daily living, or they need supervision due to cognitive impairments. Those with cognitive impairments must have evidenced that their decisions, if made independently, may jeopardize their safety or well-being or the safety of others. Family Care Homes are adult care homes that provide care to two to six unrelated residents.

In North Carolina we are able to search the internet to see the problems found at every Skilled Nursing Home when the state made their inspection. The internet has a wealth of information about facilities in the area of North Carolina. You can find a listing of for all Skilled Nursing Facilities. There is also a web site that has the list of Adult Care facilities that have special care units. Do a search for your own area and you may be able to find similar information.

There are four things to make sure you do when making a decision as to which place is the best fit for the person.[13]

1. Tour the Facility

A tour of the facility that you are considering allows you to take a first-hand look at different aspects of the physical environment such as cleanliness. It also gives you a chance to speak with staff and residents about the care and services offered at the facility to help you decide if it's the right fit for you or your loved one. While you are there, ask to see the facility's inspection reports, including any reports from the county department of social services and from the state. Facilities are required to make inspection reports from the past 12 months available to residents and families and prospective residents and families upon request.

2. Contact your local county Department of Social Services (DSS)

The county DSS adult services staffs visit each adult care facility at least quarterly throughout the year and are a good source of current information. Ask your local DSS adult home specialist about the care and services provided, as well as any recent complaints made against the facility.

3. Contact your Local Regional Long-Term Care Ombudsmen

Regional Long-Term Care Ombudsmen are advocates for residents in long-term care facilities. They provide guidance to residents and families on long-term care options in their area, how to select a long-term care facility that fits your needs and preferences, and provide information on Medicare and Medicaid programs. Ombudsmen can also provide information on the care provided in the facilities in their area, as well as recent complaints.

4. Contact the Division of Health Service Regulation, Adult Care Licensure Section

Adult care homes are licensed and inspected in North Carolina by the Division of Health Service Regulation (DHSR), Adult Care Licensure Section (ACLS). To request a copy of a facility's most recent inspection, send an email to: DHSR.AdultCare.Questions@lists.ncmail.net. You can also search on Department of Health and Human Services within your state to find out the requirements for licensing and inspection.

Hospice or No Hospice

When the word hospice is mentioned to patients or their families for many there is a dreaded fear. The thought is that hospice is just for those who only have a short time to live. Although the physician must certify that based on the medical teams best judgment the life expectancy is six months or less. The patient must have agreed to no more 'curative' treatments such as hemodialysis, chemotherapy, or radiation therapy. They now request what is called comfort care only, which means they have chosen to live out their lives as naturally and with as much comfort as possible. Those who have made the decision to go with hospice earlier than later tend to do well and live longer than the medical team's predictions. This is confirmed by a study done by the National Hospice and Palliative Care

Organizations.[19] The study found that of 4,493 terminally ill patients who elected to have hospice lived an average of one month longer than similar patients that did not have hospice services. Most of the services that hospices provide are done in the person's personal residence. They can also go to a family members home, provide care in adult care, family care and skilled nursing homes. If needed hospice can also provide care in the hospital. From my thirty three years experience in home care, I found that Christians must have a hospice that has chaplains that are Christians.[18] Look for a hospice that emphasizes what you and your loved ones needs and concerns are. The goal of hospice is to make the last of your last days the best days they can be. They should be offering emotional, spiritual and social support. Assist with the paperwork which will be detailed in the next sections. Educate about the ways to control pain and what to expect as the illness progresses. One of the most valuable service I found when my family members had hospice was the volunteers that visited and gave relief. They were there when no one else could come and were a comfort to the family when they were no longer needed for hospice services.

Final Plans

No one wants talk about death or dying. Many fear death. Even those who profess to know Jesus as their savior may still get quiet when it comes to thinking about the possibility of death, and dying. They just need to be reminded that we who are saved by the grace of Jesus do not die; only our bodies go back to the dirt from where they were formed by God.

John 3:36 He that believeth on the Son hath everlasting life: and he that believeth not the Son shall not see life; but the wrath of God abideth on him.

The plans that need to be made are funeral arrangements, details about what will happen, where and who will do the ceremony. All of us should have discussed these subjects with our loved ones while we are healthy and of sound mind. Write out the details that have importance to you. Think about the costs of completed your plans. Do you have insurance? How much of the final expenses will it cover? If you do not know go by the local funeral homes in your area if you have not picked out the one you would like. Ask them the cost of the type of service you had in mind. If you really do not have any preferences then just let your family know this also.

There are three other documents that everyone needs to consider completing before they become too ill or mentally unable to decisions. These forms are part of the Advance Directives.

These directives pertain to treatment preferences and the designation of a surrogate decision-maker in the event that a person should become unable to make medical decisions on their own behalf. Advance directives generally fall into three categories: living will, power of attorney and health care proxy.[13]

LIVING WILL: This is a written document that specifies what types of medical treatment are desired. A living will can be very specific or very general. The most common statement in a living will is to the effect that: If I suffer an incurable, irreversible illness, disease, or condition and my attending physician determines that my condition is terminal, I direct that life-sustaining measures that would serve only to prolong my dying be withheld or discontinued. More specific living wills may include information regarding an individual's desire for such services such as analgesia (pain relief), antibiotics, hydration, feeding, and the use of ventilators or cardiopulmonary resuscitation.[14]

HEALTH CARE PROXY: This is also called a Health Care Power of Attorney. This is a legal document in which an individual designates another person to make health care decisions if he or she is rendered incapable of making their wishes known. The health care proxy has, in essence, the same rights to request or refuse treatment that the individual would have if capable of making and communicating decisions.[14]

DURABLE POWER OF ATTORNEY: This is the third type of advance directive. Individuals may draft legal documents providing power of attorney to others in the case of incapacitating medical condition. The durable power of attorney allows an individual to make bank transactions, sign Social Security checks, apply for disability, or simply write checks to pay the utility bill while an individual is medically incapacitated.[14]

When creating your Living Will, Health Care Power of Attorney or Durable Power of Attorney think about who you are designating as the person who will make decisions for you and your money. You will be in no position to argue if they do not do as you wish. So talk to the person you would like to designate to see if they in your best judgment will be impartial and will not let your family sway the decisions you have made. The person you designate does not have to be a relative. Just pick someone who will be on the same page as you are. I created my Living will and health care power of attorney and durable power of attorney when I had my first surgery at age thirty. I did not do it because I thought I would die, I did it because I knew there was a chance I could be on a ventilator as a part of my surgery at post –op and I wanted to be very clear about how long I was to be on the ventilator. I had a long discussion with my family physician and my sister who I designated. I asked her many questions until I was satisfied that she would make the decision I would want. I am also confident that she will consult the Lord about any decision she would have to make.

What about DNR orders or wishes? North Carolina's Right to a Natural Death Act recognizes a patient's right to a peaceful and natural death. It outlines an optional and nonexclusive procedure for respecting this right that provides a safe harbor of protection from liability in circumstances involving withholding or withdrawing extraordinary means of life support or artificial nutrition or hydration from an incompetent patient who is terminally and incurably ill, comatose or in a persistent vegetative state.[13] The statute defines "extraordinary means" as "any medical procedure or intervention which in the judgment of the attending physician would serve only to postpone artificially the moment of death by sustaining, restoring, or supplanting a vital function." Since "extraordinary means" refers to "any medical procedure or intervention," it encompasses CPR in circumstances where the physician has determined that this intervention would serve only to postpone artificially the moment of death.[12]

One more document that is forgotten by most people is a will. A will is a legal document that describes how a person wants his property divided upon his death.[12] A will can only be made by an adult who is of sound mind at the time of creating the will. A will is a private personnel document. Many families have become divided because of the division of property in a will. We tend to forget what the will represents. How the person who wrote the will feel about the one he left his possessions to. To be legal a will must be signed in the presence of two witnesses. Any person competent to be a witness in a court of law may act as a witness to a will.[12]

Before discussing end of life wishes with others, here are some tips to use prior to having this tough conversation.

- Start with yourself. Take the forms and complete them for yourself. This helps you think about the decisions that need to be made. The conflicts that make it difficult to make a decision about some areas.

- Do not change the way in which you have been communicating with the person. If you have only talked to them with a family member or on the phone then have this conversation using the same method.

- Choose the time and place. Make a special appointment to discuss this. Let the person know you would like to discuss some forms with them such as a will, living will, final arrangement wishes. This way they are prepared to listen and have a discussion about these things.

- Anticipate the reactions and prepare for your responses. Remember your reactions as you prepared your forms.

- Do not delay having this conversation with those who have been the most difficult during this time. They need to know sooner so they can adjust to this difficult task.

- Rely on the peers in your ministerial group or your church. Go discuss with those who have been doing this for a while. Home Health and Hospice chaplains, medical social workers, and nurses are good resources. Many will talk over the phone with you. Look in the phone directory for your local organization.

- Investigate the law within your state and consult an attorney to be sure you have the proper documentation.

We all know we need to do these forms and make preparations but we usually don't do them all.

To find resources in your local area search for the following:

Skilled Nursing Facilities/Senior Care

Adult Care facilities with Special Needs

Living Will Form/Desire for Natural Death

Power of Attorney Forms

A resource for making the decisions required on these forms is Hard Choices for Loving People, Fourth edition, by Hank Dunn, Chaplain, www.hardchoices.com[19]

Chapter VIII

Care to Those Left Behind

The last section I want to cover is on care to those in the season of grief. The purpose of ministry for this season of life is to assist the person to adjust to a different daily life. Grief is a deeply personal experience, a normal, natural response to death and loss. The duration for this period can be days, weeks, months, years or decades. Every person goes through this period differently. The same person can react differently when grieving at different times.

It's a personal thing.

Dr. Elisabeth Kübler-Ross, is a renown psychiatrist that did an in depth study of the grief process. Her book, "On Death and Dying "is a required reading in many Medical, Nursing and Divinity Schools throughout the United States. For her research she interviewed with more than 500 dying patients.[35] Based on the results of her interviews she developed what is known as the five stages of grief. These stages are not to be regarded as complete or in chronological order. I put this discussion on this chapter because we tend to associate these stages with those who are that are left still living as well as those who are dying. Dr. Ross's theory brought awareness to the sensitivity required for better treatment of individuals who are dealing with terminal illness and end-stage of life. Her theory about the stages of grieve soon expanded to apply to any form of catastrophic personal loss (job, income, freedom) as well as significant life events such as the death of a loved one, major rejection, end of a relationship, the onset of a disease or chronic illness, diagnosis, as well many tragedies and disasters.

The five stages are:

1. **Denial** — Denial is usually only a temporary defense mechanism for the individual. When a

person is in this stage you may hear responses or actions that portray the person does not believe they are in the end stage of illness. They may deny they even have an illness. They may refuse to have anyone say the name of the illness or anything related to it. When a person is in this stage it is not a "bad thing". It is where they are. For the faith community this stage can be seen as a faith statement. And in many cases it can be. It can also hinder the person when it is prolonged from appropriate treatment or comfort measures.

2. **Anger** — This defense mechanism is easily identified. The person in this stage displays all the ways they get angry. If they yelled when they get angry, then the yelling is louder and can be directed at the person who is the closest to them. Many times the anger is at God. The words of anger to God are never pleasant to hear. Some will apologize as soon

as they say the words, yet many others will not. They may try to justify their right to say these things because of their good deeds. The chapter of Job is a good place to direct them. When they are ready to listen. You have to use your gift of discernment to know the correct time to respond. But rest assured if it is not the correct time, you will know by the angry outbursts directed at you. Eventually the individual recognizes that denial cannot continue. This is the time that your ministry to the caregivers needs to increase. During the stage of anger, the person is very difficult to care for due to misplaced feelings of rage and envy most of the time aimed at the caregiver. .

3. **Bargaining** —The third stage involves the hope that the individual can somehow postpone or delay death. Usually, the negotiation for an extended life is made with a higher power in exchange for a

reformed lifestyle. Psychologically, the individual is saying, "I understand I will die, but if I could just do something to buy more time..."

4. **Depression** — During the fourth stage, the dying person begins to understand the certainty of death. Because of this, the individual may become silent, refuse visitors and spend much of the time crying and grieving. This process allows the dying person to disconnect from things of love and affection. It is not recommended to attempt to cheer up an individual who is in this stage. It is an important time for grieving that must be processed.

5. **Acceptance** —In this last stage, individuals begin to come to terms with their mortality, or that of a loved one, or other tragic event. This is the stage of these type of comments: "It's going to be okay"

There is another stage left out of this model that is an important one for the faith community to be aware of:

Loneliness – This stage is usually seen between depression and acceptance. It can also be a major player during the depression stage.

Not everyone who experiences a life-threatening or life-altering event goes through all of these stages. Those who do experience them will do not have them in any particular order. Reactions to illness, death, and loss are as unique as the person experiencing them. Some people may get stuck in one stage.

The opportunities for the faith community to show the caring spirit of Christ exists at every stage of grief. By reviewing the emotional, physical and spiritual needs for a person in grief you can find a way you can be of help.[16]

Emotional Needs: To express their feelings no matter how bad they seem, they need to accept help, they need to ask for help that friends do not provide, be kind to themselves. Do the activities they enjoyed before the loss.

Physical Needs: Lots of good rest, to have peaceful sleep, stay healthy by eating and taking meds if required, be alert for clinical depression.

Spiritual Needs: That God has not forgotten them. That their faith community still loves them. That weeping may endure for a night, but joy *cometh* in the morning. Psalms: 30:5b

What can we do? Be a great listener. Do not say things like: Don't cry your know Mother would not like, that it negates and diminishes the value of the life loss. Never compare someone's reaction to this death by how they reacted the last time. What about this statement: I know what you are going through; I lost my sister 6 months ago. What's wrong with saying this you don't know what that person is going through, what if she did not get along with her mother and you and your sister were best friends. When you don't know what to say, don't say anything. Give a hug, a hand squeeze, take out the trash, or wash a dish. Assist with cards and letters. Answer the telephone. Encourage independence; eat meals with them so they eat better. Serve and minister. When in grief we all must acknowledge the death, and experience the pain. The way I deal with pain and the way you deal with pain will be different. Please don't ask how are you? You know they cannot be in the greatest of moods. Don't just be there to hear the sad story. Be there to lift those in mourning up not drag them down. Be there to help them remember the happy times with their loved one. They have the images of the hospital and the sad things front and center.

During the time of grief a person can show anger at small things. An object or special belonging of the departed moved an inch from the way it was can trigger a response. Someone sitting in their chair or in the favorite spot can trigger anger that is not explained. Do not argue. Do not say it is o.k., just quietly ask the person who is the subject of anger to relocate.

During grief the one in pain may "talk "to the person. As we minister to those in grief pray for discernment so you can tell when the normal reactions turn to abnormal ones. Many like to just talk of their loved ones, look at pictures, read old letters etc.; just be there and listen. Sometimes the person is alone for the first time in many years. They now have a big change in their routine.

When my two best friends died close in time to each other I was like a fish out of water, I felt like I was suffocating in my own home.[22] We were like the three musketeers. We did so much together. I was lost without my running buddies to laugh with, go eat with, go to the movies, and other activities. My former co-worker Robin a medical social worker for home health and hospice, found out both my buddies had passed. She called to express her sorrow and love for me. She wanted to take me to dinner. The more I said no the more she talked about how she admired the way I helped her during a loss. Then she would ask me about another restaurant and tried to get me to say yes. She told me to check my calendar and she would call me in two days. She did not wait for two days. She called the next day, a Friday night, and stated she had somewhere for us to go and she would be there in thirty minutes, just throw on a pair of jeans. Robin knew this was just what my friends would do. I went out in remembrance of them. I really enjoyed myself. Robin gave me the time to talk about them both and she just listened and let me cry, laugh and be me.

Robin made these surprise social events for me for about six months. Robin scheduled the activities that I told her "the three musketeers" did during our talk that first night. I was feeling like my old self again and she decreased the frequency until my life was busy again. She withdrew because she knew I was whole again.

As you minster to those in grief resolve some of the misguided things you may have assumed. Crying or not crying, are both normal responses. It just depends on the person. It is not necessarily a sign of problems. Children need to grieve. Just remember the information about children discussed earlier. Do not avoid discussing the loss with a grieving person. Those who grieve are grateful to share memories and talk about the pain their loss created. The love for the person that passed does not end when the grieving period is over.

When the grieving person has blamed God or has not returned to church services our job as the community of faith is to guide them back to God. We need to let them know the times when we are the least in control is when we need to affirm that God is still with us. Sometimes God is blamed for not healing or for taking the person form them. This is not a time to condemn the statements or the feelings. Just as we forgive each other we must help the person in forgiving themselves for the anger at God. Gently remind them through the scriptures of how God has not left them. Show them the goodness of the master by the actions of the church. Go get pick them up for the service. Specially invite them back to service. Make them feel missed and valuable to the body of Christ. There is a technique that hospice uses to minister to those during the acute period of grief. This technique helps to enrich the prayer life and led to closeness to God.

Assist them to pray their memories of their loved one as they go through the acute phase of grief. Think on a memory about the person who has passed. Think of holding the memory in the palm of your hand. Securely wrap both hands around the memory and imagine placing it in a beautiful gift box. Then in your mind's eye, place the gift box in the hands of God. God is now embracing the memory with you. Begin praying to Him as you give the gift box, thanking the Lord for the gift of that memory. This is also a way to release the disturbing memories left from the hospital or other distressing time. Look up scriptures that may be a help prior to the prayer starting.

Isaiah 26: 3-4 Thou wilt keep *him* in perfect peace, *whose* mind *is* stayed *on thee*: because he trusteth in thee. Trust ye in the LORD for ever: for in the LORD JEHOVAH *is* everlasting strength:

Throughout the scriptures they prayed their memories.

Isaiah 38:3 Then Hezekiah turned his face toward the wall, and prayed unto the LORD, And said, Remember now, O LORD, I beseech thee, how I have walked before thee in truth and with a perfect heart, and have done *that which is* good in thy sight. And Hezekiah wept sore.

Philippians 1:3-6 I thank my God upon every remembrance of you, Always in every prayer of mine for you all making request with joy, For your fellowship in the gospel from the first day until now;

Being confident of this very thing, that he which hath begun a good work in you will perform *it* until the day of Jesus Christ:

Our memories are God given treasures that become precious companions during times of grief. By assisting others to pray their memories you help them experience

God's wisdom, grace, and revelation in the history of their life.

Questions for Remembering

- When you think of _____ what words best describe his personality?

- Tell me a story that you feel shows this about _____.

- How do you want people to remember _____.

- What were ___ favorite scriptures, song, movies, tv shows. [17]

Some churches have developed a grief support list. They check off tasks that the family needs. If their faith community is not able to supply all the needs, they coordinate with the other groups associated with the bereaved family. The following is a sample list.[2]

Before or during the funeral or memorial service:

- Going with family members to the funeral home to make final arrangements

- Stay at the central home to answer the phone, take in food or flowers, run errands, light housekeeping

- Assess what staple foods and paper are needed and get them

- Recording the gifts, and phone calls received

- Arranging transportation for out of town family, to and from air port

- Hosting out of town guests

- Watching/entertaining children

- Assist with the care of pets

- Provide a light breakfast or lunch prior to the funeral or memorial service

- Coordinate the after service meal for family and friends

Immediately following the funeral or memorial service:

- Assist with the clean up at the home

- Transportation of out of town guests

- Calling to check in during the next few days and weeks

- Help with thank you cards

- Help returning dishes and other items

- Offering to bring dinner to drop off or share

- Offering to transport the grieving family to worship

- Helping with light housekeeping or yard work

- Helping with paperwork and required filings

- Assist in transporting to the required agencies to file needed paperwork[3]

Get together with your ministering group and formulate your unique list to meet the needs of those you will minister to. Here is a poem I want you to remember as you

council, visit and remember those in grief. It was written by
an unknown author who had lost a young child to cancer.

Say My Child's Name

The mention of my child's name

May bring tears to my eyes,

But it never fails

to bring music to my ears.

If you are really my friend,

Let me hear the music of her name!

It soothes my broken heart

And sings to my soul![3]

The grieving period after the funeral or memorial service is
over can become a life threatening condition. The support
of the faith community can be the difference in the eventual
recovery of the mourner. Get in touch on the phone to see
when to come over. The sooner is the better. Say little on

the first visit, your embrace, touch a quick I love you, I am here for you, is enough.

Avoid the clichés. The "he's out of pain; it is a blessing he did not linger" are not helpful but hurtful. It makes it sound like the person's life should have been shortened and ripped from them. A simple I am saddened by your loss, I am here for you is enough. Lift the burden off the person in the small ways. A person who was an immaculate housekeeper will not be and may be embarrassed by the condition of her home. Go about assisting without fanfare. Make it seem like that is why you came to serve her. They do not feel like talking, then be silent. Just sit there. Do not ask questions about the illness or death. I they want to talk about it just listen. Do not discuss the trivial news of your life even if they ask, a simple I am fine I came to help you. Avoid pity, and a constant reminder of the loss. Encourage postponing major decisions. Explain that they have plenty of time to decide later. Ministering during the period of grief can help both the griever and the ministry group grow

in grace, health and spirituality.

SUMMARY

Providing support to those with chronic, terminal or end stage illnesses is a ministry we sometimes over look. Those of us who do minister to this group are not doing all we could do to assure they are getting their spiritual needs met. Those who are grieving need our help to find their way to a different existence. When you have lost a loved one you have lost the life you knew. It is our job as the faith community to lead them to their changed life with love. Here are some final guidelines to use to plan your own strategy to take care of these hurting groups.

Offer support by just being there. Normalize their feelings, whatever they are feeling is a part of the process to wholeness. Listen without an agenda; just be an ear for them to express the contents of their hearts. Be the educator for resources, contacts and needed information. Encourage the use of helpers without guilt. Remember the anniversaries they will now have. Send a thoughtful but not morose card or call or even better go see them. Take them out to a remembering place.

A final thought: helping must be more than following a few rules. This is especially true if you are close to the bereaved. You may have to give more time, cancel some things on your schedule, and sacrifice a few things. It will require more time, more of yourself, and more care than you ever imagined. The perception needed to anticipate the special needs of the bereaved and creatively meet those needs will be tremendous. Such commitment is rare.

Matthew 9:37 Then saith he unto his disciples, The harvest truly *is* plenteous, but the labourers *are* few; Pray ye therefore the Lord of the harvest, that he will send forth labourers into his harvest.

Luke 10:2 Therefore said he unto them, The harvest truly *is* great, but the labourers *are* few: pray ye therefore the Lord of the harvest, that he would send forth labourers into his harvest.

The Charge to the Faith Community

Extend Immediate Support	Give Extended Support
Develop a Plan	Relate Fond Memories
Become Educated	Companionship

What do we need to do?

JUST BE THERE!

BIBLIOGRAPHY/REFERENCES

1. Matthew Henry's Commentary on the New Testament

2. The Unbroken Circle: A Tool kit for Congregations Around Illness, End of Life and Greif

3. James L. Brooks, M.Div.

4. The 36 Hour Day, 4th Edition   Nancy L. Mace MD, Peter V.Rabins, MD, MPH

5. Doing Well at Being Sick   Wendy Wallace

6. American Reformed Christian   Jay. E. Adams

7. The Portable Caregiver   Mary Trabert, www.mettajourney.com

8. Coping with Chronic Pain   Care Notes, Sefra Kobtin Pitzele

9. Praying with Someone Sick or Confined Charles Meyer

10. Sick Girl Speaks: Lessons and Ponderings Along the Road to Acceptance

11. Tiffany Christiansen: www.sickgirlspeaks.com

12. Susan G. Koman for the Cure Foundation http://ww5.komen.org

13. Cancer in Woman: Western Schools Home Study 2nd Edition; revised by Suzanne M. Maburn, RN

14. North Carolina Statues www.ncga.state.nc.us/gascripts/Statues

15. NC Department of Health and Human Resources www.NCDHHS.gov/dhsr

16. US Legal. Inc   www.uslegal.com

17. Gone From My Sight the Dying Experience Barbara Karnes

BIBLIOGRAPHY/REFERENCES (continued)

18. CareNotes   Abbey Press

19. UNC Hospice   Gail Smith,
    Chaplain, Andrea Tuttle, MSW

20. Hard Choices for Loving People   Hank Dunn,
    Chaplain

21. The National Hospice and palliative Care Organization
    www.nhpco.org

22. The Hundreds of patients, their family members, and
    caregivers that forced me to continually grow in this
    area of service to others.

23. My dear friend Rilla Vanhook who gave me the
    opportunity to release the fear of being around those
    who are at physical death.

24. My beloved friend, Marion Lacewell who helped me to
    understand the pain and needs of those who experience
    a sudden death.

25. My friends, family, faith community that accept the gift
    of receiving care when I needed it.

26. The Oxford English Dictionary
    www.oxforddictionary.com

27. Web-MD www.webmd.com

28. Grief Ministry   Donna Reilly Williams and JoAnn
    Sturzl

29. Bishop Larry Jackson   Bethel Outreach International
    Church, Charlotte NC

30. The News and Observer   Raleigh NC

31. Annette Williams, AbleAnnie Administrative
    www.ableannie.com

BIBLIOGRAPHY/REFERENCES (continued)

32. Elder J. Stephen Williams,The Laying on of Hands

33. Competent to Council   Jay E. Adams

34. Wikipedia www.Wikipedia.com

35. National Cancer Institute
         www.nationalcancerinstitute.org

35. Dying Well   Dr. Ira Bylock

36. On Death and Dying   Dr. Elizabeth Kubler-Ross